EMPATHY

EMPATHY

ITS NATURE
AND USES

Robert L. Katz

THE FREE PRESS OF GLENCOE

COLLIER-MACMILLAN LIMITED, LONDON

To
Mimi
and our children
Amy Jean, Michael, and Jonathan

PREFACE

EMPATHY IS A rich, puzzling, and intriguing phenomenon. Experts in the arts, the sciences, and the helping professions are far from satisfied with what they know about the origin of empathy, its nature, and its variations. Each field of specialization has a contribution to make to our understanding, but often the specialist speaks only to his peers. Communication across the disciplines and the professions should be opened up so that we can pool what insights we have about the meaning and operation of empathy. Our subject could easily engage the joint efforts of a panel of experts, each competent to illumine some facet of empathy. My goal in this book is to select, focus, and interpret insights from such apparently divergent fields as aesthetics, biology, sociology, and psychoanalysis. A single observer who reviews and organizes materials has the opportunity of formulating hypotheses which in turn can be examined at leisure by specialists in terms of the growing edges of their own technical knowledge.

This book deals with the uses as well as the nature of empathy. A study of the operations of empathy helps us understand its essence. Both the more general student and the professional worker in human relations need to appreciate the distinction between simple or raw empathy and the sophisticated dialectic of subjective involvement and objective scrutiny which we call "empathic understanding." When we analyze empathic processes in the counseling or therapeutic situation, we gain some clues about the personal creativity of the empathizer, we become more aware of the effects of empathy upon the object as well as the subject, and we appreciate more clearly the factors that correlate positively with successful empathic communication.

My exposition of the role of empathy is occasionally punctuated with judgmental asides, which represent my own suggestions, as a nonspecialist, concerning the more creative use of empathy. Practitioners of empathy other than psychotherapists—psychologists, caseworkers, physicians, clergymen, and marriage counselors—may discover unsuspected dimensions of their own empathic involvement and come to appreciate more sharply the risks as well as the potential gains of their empathic activity. The issue concerning an empathic variable among therapists should be of interest. The material in this book should be of value to those whose aim is simply an increase in understanding of human psychology. It would be of value for those who have some variety of counseling relationship. It could have value to those who do psychotherapy, for it is the material from psychotherapy which has been most relevant as grist for the mill of our understanding of empathic phenomena. Only incidental reference is made to the considerable literature about empathy and socioempathy in social psychology and in sociometry. I have been concerned with the dynamics of empathy rather than with the *measurement* of empathy among group members or with the identification of common traits and simple like or dislike responses. I have concentrated on empathy as a process or encounter between individuals. In considering the uses of empathy I have focused on its applications to the counseling or therapeutic relationship rather than on its relevance for solving problems and mediating tensions among minorities, social classes, communities, or peoples.

The following chapters concerned with the applications of empathy do not deal with such essential features of counseling or psychotherapy as diagnosis and clinical understanding. Empathy is a part but not the whole of the helping process. Each counseling or therapeutic specialty has its own repertory of techniques and professional resources appropriate to its interests and treatment objectives. My primary concern is with empathy and its relevance to a variety of professions. I stress its importance and argue that a clearer understanding of its functions will add to its potential usefulness in more than one way.

Problems of terminology abound in an eclectic study. This applies to the working vocabulary of the psychoanalyst, the caseworker, and the more general counselor, in addition to being a problem in moving from the frame of reference of one science to another. Some awkwardness is inevitable in the language of a book addressed to a heterogeneous audience. I am not consistent in the use of such terms as therapist, counselor, patient, or client. I do not mean to imply that the work done by the psychoanalyst and the counselor is of a piece, and I make no recommendations for changing the domains of the psychoanalyst, the therapist, and the counselor. Anyone who takes the role of a helper in psychological and subjective concerns of other people is confronted with the complexities of empathic involvement no matter what level of depth the relationship takes. Some relationships are more emotionally charged than others, but proficiency in empathy is almost always expected of the helping person if he is a professional and responsible individual. Psychoanalysts, physicians, and counselors, for example, do not enter into the same relationship with the individuals they help; but empathy is a common denominator among them. Such a common denominator by no means deprives each specialty of its uniqueness. If readers recognize that this is a book about empathy, not a manual on technique for any particular profession, they may find the present usage more tolerable.

Case discussions are not included. Practitioners of empathy can find examples illustrating varieties of empathy by scrutinizing their own work. The reference in Chapter II to a phase of a counseling interview illustrates the steps in empathic understanding and is not offered as an example of technique. I refer the reader to Theodor Reik's *Listening with the Third Ear* for a detailed account of empathic processes as experienced by a veteran psychoanalyst. I deal with the *concept* of empathy and with the principles of its operation. Apart from a few polemics in the first and last chapters, I believe I have written soberly and objectively about a subjective process. I have been interested in a logical exposition of a skill which itself is nonverbal and nonlogical.

Since my understanding of empathic phenomena has been stimulated and nourished by published statements of different specialists, I have included quotations from authorities in the body of the text. Detailed information concerning the works quoted can be found in the reference section. Items which have not been quoted directly but which are significant for students of empathy are listed in the bibliography. Works which have been particularly helpful, in addition to the volume by Reik, are Max Scheler's *The Nature of Sympathy* and an article by Carter Zelesnik, "The Role of Empathy in Science, Measurement, and Control" (1957). My own earlier publication in this area was an article published in 1959 entitled "Empathy in Modern Psychotherapy and in the Aggada."

I wish to express special thanks to Dr. Nelson Glueck, President of the Hebrew Union College-Jewish Institute of Religion, not only for encouraging this particular study but also for initiating the department of Human Relations and facilitating my scholarly and teaching programs. Dr. Samuel Sandmel has been consistently helpful. I deeply appreciate the suggestions offered by my former colleague, Dr. Henry D. Lederer, as I was outlining the project and writing the first draft. My colleagues, Drs. Sheldon H. Blank, Stanley L. Block, and Elias L. Epstein read the manuscript patiently. I thank them, my student Norman Mirsky, and Mr. Thomas Simpson and Miss Marlene Mandel of The Free Press for editorial comments. Mrs. Helen Lederer typed with care and has earned my appreciation. My wife's empathy provided both insight and support.

ROBERT L. KATZ

Cincinnati, Ohio
January, 1963

CONTENTS

EMPATHY

I

EMPATHY AND THE
COUNSELING ROLES

THE TERM "empathy" has become a part of the working vocabulary of our age. It is familiar to laymen as well as to philosophers, psychologists, sociologists, and to members of the helping professions. "Sympathetic imagination" and "sympathetic understanding" are close synonyms. It is generally and somewhat loosely taken to refer to nonverbal communication and to the apprehension of inner emotional states. It suggests a somewhat odd and elusive skill, a divinatory art, a sixth sense, an instinctive and primitive form of penetrating to the core of another person. It has been said that "to empathize is to see with the eyes of another, to hear with the ears of another, and to feel with the heart of another." (Anonymous English author as quoted by Alfred Adler.)

The modern use of the term dates from the year 1897, when

the German psychologist Theodor Lipps published a description of a process of aesthetic appreciation. He used the term *Einfühlung* to designate losing self-awareness on the part of an observer as he confronts a painting or a piece of sculpture and a tendency of the subject to fuse with the object that absorbs his attention. Edward B. Titchener of Cornell introduced "empathy" as an English equivalent for the original German.

Familiar as the term may be, we are far from having a clear understanding of what empathy really is. This is not a particular concern of the layman, unless empathy as a phenomenon of everyday experience excites his curiosity. Those who have an academic or scientific interest in processes of communication have debated long but inconclusively about empathy as a cognitive technique which may be innate, acquired, or both. The meaning of empathy, its origin, and its use challenge specialists in the social sciences who use subjective methods to investigate the inner meaning of various cultures. Counselors, psychologists, and therapists use empathy in their professional practice, sometimes to make diagnoses and often to establish helping relationships, and therefore want to comprehend its exact nature more fully and to determine what can be achieved through the disciplined use of empathy as a tool in professional practice. They are neither satisfied with the knowledge they now have of empathy nor sufficiently confident about where and how empathy should be used.

Empathy is so pervasive and so puzzling a phenomenon that any exploration of its nature and its uses must include insights from a variety of disciplines. Specialists analyze and interpret empathy in their own frames of reference; the interrelations among these theories of empathy have not been fully recognized and appreciated. One of our goals is to identify what common core, if any, can be found among the data and inferences available in several sciences. We intend to examine the connotation of empathy in biology as a form of instinctive reverberation, its definition in psychoanalytic theory as a form of identification, its equation in social psychology with experimental role-taking and in sociology as mutual understanding among members of the same in-group. We shall consider the implications of the psychologist's and psychiatrist's use of empathy as an index of the mental and emotional status of the patient. A major focus of our attention will be empathy as a subjective process in the counselor or the therapist and its application in human relations. We must be eclectic in our approach because insights concerning the meaning and function of empathy abound in the sciences and the humanities. No single source, not even one as significant as psychoanalysis, should be expected to account fully for the phenomenon of empathy in human relations.

Empathy and Everyman

When we experience empathy, we feel as if we were experiencing someone else's feelings as our own. We see, we feel, we respond, and we understand as if we were, in fact, the other person. We stand in his shoes. We get under his skin. Often we are not unaware of our empathizing. Sometimes we directly ask the other person to empathize with us, as when we ask, "what would you do if you were me?" More often than not, however, we take the part of the other person and expect him to take ours without being aware of our own activities or our expectations of others.

When we take the position of another person, our imagination projects us out of ourselves and into the other person. We may experience certain changes in our own muscles and actual physical posture. Our involvement with others becomes physical when we imitate their gestures and follow the movement of their bodies with our own. Watching a basketball game, we lose ourselves in the action on the court. Without any conscious effort on our part, our muscles tense as the guard leaps upward to block a basket. Our bodies react to the excitement of the contest as though we ourselves were on the court, straining to make a point for our own team. We also take part in the physical tension of our fellow spectators. When they jump up to cheer, we are caught up in the contagious excitement and jump to our feet. We become one with the feelings and actions of our neighbors. When we are passengers in a car, we press on the floor in a moment of physically experienced empathy with the driver. We

yawn when our neighbors yawn. When we are seated in the
theater, tears come to our eyes and we feel agitated and depressed
when we feel within ourselves the movements and gestures of
an actor whose own part we have been playing. We are in the
audience and on the stage at the same time.

To empathize does not mean that the individual must experience physical sensations; empathy can be physical, imaginative,
or both. Even when it is "imaginative," it is more than "intellectual." With or without identifiable organic sensations, empathy
still connotes a form of personal involvement and an evocation
of feeling. Our empathy is no less real if our bodies undergo no
physical change and if we move into the situation of the other
person only in our fantasy. We experience internal sensations
and responses, even though we may be unable to specify the
particular part of the body where the sensation might be located.
In everyday experience our empathic involvement may include
either imaginative or somatic responses or both. Our imaginative
powers propel us into the position of the people with whom we
feel identified.

We have all had the sense of genuine participation in the experience of the other person, even if this experience takes place
in our mind's eye, as it were. The husband imagines what his wife
must be feeling at a particular moment because he is able to see
and hear in his own fantasy as if he were standing in his wife's
shoes and is for the moment experiencing her own situation.
When a person empathizes he abandons himself and relives in
himself the emotions and responses of another person. He is
capable of experiencing in himself a mood that is so analogous
to the mood of the other person as to represent the exact feelings
of the other person quite closely. He remains an individual in
his own right with his own private experiences, but in moments
of empathy he experiences the keenest and most vivid sense of
closeness or sameness with the other person.

We tend to think of empathy as a reaction to the stimulus of
personal contact with the other person. In a face-to-face encounter we feel the contagion of the attitudes and feelings of
the other person. We automatically respond in a kind of imitative activity. At times this is an inner imitation; at other times it

amounts to a physical sensation and may reveal itself in our gestures or in our facial expression. Our response is triggered by cues in the conversation or by impressions we receive of the state of mind or feeling of the other person. We assimilate this information without being aware of doing so. We pick up the signals through a kind of inner radar and certain changes in our own emotional states make themselves felt. We mimic the other person and in the excitement of our spontaneous response our attention is almost completely absorbed. For the moment the vicarious experience grips us. We reverberate to the emotions of the other person and are no longer aware of our separate identity. We are involved in *as-if* behavior. We become self-forgetful. Abandoning our own self, we seem to become fused with and absorbed in the inner experience of the other person.

Sometimes the contagion which evokes our empathy comes from personal contact with people we perceive and confront, but some forms of empathy can also be evoked by the stimulus of the written word. The student who reads the speech given by Socrates before his execution is transported to ancient Greece and inwardly prepares to drink the cup along with the heroic philosopher. The historian who pores over the newspaper accounts of the Civil War recaptures the situation of the time "as it actually was." "The past," writes Louis Gottschalk, "can be incorporated into the living memory of the historian, becoming almost as real to him as his own past" (1945, p. 67). It is possible to empathize with individuals or characters who are themselves the products of the artist's imagination. Mark Twain conjures up the figure of Tom Sawyer and elaborates his characterization through empathy. Succeeding generations of readers then empathize with the fictional character. Even before appearing on the stage and physically enacting the drama, the actor empathizes with the role which was originally the product of the playwright's imagination.

With whom do we easily empathize in everyday experience? Usually it is with those who are close to us personally. We empathize with relatives, with friends, with others who are like us and who have had similar experiences. We appreciate the sufferings and conflicts of others who, like ourselves, cannot control their need to drink and seek help in groups like Alcoholics Anonymous. We empathize with our Negro fellows because we experience the same social rejection. If we are teen-agers we have a language of our own and a special feeling for the appetites and dreams of our peers. If we are Jews we often have an almost natural empathy with other Jews. We share a common history and destiny and appreciate the role of the Jew despite certain differences in cultural background, religious pattern, or citizenship. The husband and wife who have long experienced the give and take of married life often enjoy an almost automatic empathy; one can read the mind of the other. Understanding in marriage is quick and intimate when genuine companionship has been achieved. In the case of individuals afflicted with the same disease, the appreciation of its meaning and the responses that go with it are mutual; the physician who is himself a diabetic often has a quick appreciation of the diabetic patient and his problems.

We find it more difficult to empathize with strangers, although it is not unusual to have the sudden and inexplicable sensation of empathy with a stranger whom we meet quite by chance. As members of an audience we sometimes have the uncanny feeling that the speaker understands what we are thinking and that he is communicating with us directly as if he had some personal knowledge of us and was intending his words only for us. It is not unusual to get a kind of "cold insight" into new acquaintances.

It is a matter of common experience that we find it more difficult to establish empathy with those who are different from us. If we live in a big city middle-class neighborhood, we cannot easily imagine what it would be like to live as a share cropper on some remote hillside. As professionals, we have difficulty projecting ourselves into the experiences of the milkman or the clerk in the supermarket. We are not likely to empathize easily with the monk who has taken the vows of poverty, obedience, chastity, and silence. Age differences, too, interfere with empathy. As grandfathers we have some empathy with children, but as sons or grandsons we can have less empathy with the aged for we have no personal experience of being an older person. It is almost impossible for us, if we are men, to empathize with such exclusively feminine experiences as menstruating or giving birth. We tend to empathize with those who are familiar to us or whose life situation is most similar to our own.

In some situations we would not even attempt to empathize. It is conceivable that empathy might even interfere with the conduct of our affairs. We naturally empathize when we converse about our inner attitudes and feelings, in our relationships with good friends, with relatives, and with colleagues. We have no such need when we engage in brief contacts or transactions. We do not empathize with the driver of the crowded bus nor do we anticipate that he will give us personal attention. When we exchange polite greetings in casual meetings at crowded cocktail parties, it is not likely that we will have the time or the inclination to *feel ourselves into* the private and personal environment of others. The drill sergeant who wants to whip a mob of new recruits into a marching column has no time for empathy. If we were soldiers and permitted ourselves to empathize with the enemy, we would likely be disabled as was George Orwell when fighting in Spain. His rifle was trained on an enemy soldier but he could not pull the trigger when he observed the enemy standing with his pants down. Orwell immediately identified with the man as a fellow human being and at that point became useless as a soldier. Empathy can be a distraction, too, if we take the role of judge or if we are called on to administer a policy along broad and impersonal lines.

What do we ordinarily derive from empathy? It serves us in two ways. First, it helps us to understand the other person from within. We communicate on a deeper level and apprehend the other person more completely. With this kind of communication we often find ourselves accepting that person and entering into a relationship of appreciation and sympathy. In another sense, empathy becomes for us a source of personal reassurance. We are reassured when we feel that someone has succeeded in feeling himself into our own state of mind. We enjoy the satisfaction of being understood and accepted as persons. It is important for us to sense that the other person not only understands our words but appreciates the person behind the message as well. We then know that we are recognized and accepted for the particular kind of person we are. When friends fail to empathize, we feel disappointed and rejected. We want people to listen to us empathically, even if they are familiar with what we are going to say. We look for a feeling response and when that is lacking, we feel that something is wrong with the personal relationship. The exchange of verbal messages is not always enough for us. We look for a correspondence of mood. When we find it in face-to-face meetings with friends, when we sense it in reading the words of Shakespeare or in a favorite Psalm, we are less lonely and more content. When empathy is lacking, our self-awareness and self-respect are diminished. We then experience ourselves more as objects and less as persons.

Empathy and Sympathy

When we discuss involvement in the situation of others, can we make a distinction between sympathy and empathy? There is a close connection, as the earlier use of the term "sympathetic imagination" for what we now know as empathy would indicate. It is true that in both sympathy and empathy we permit our feelings for others to become involved. The purpose of the two activities are different, however. In empathy we focus our attention on the feelings and the situation of the other person. In Gardner Murphy's terms, it is "experiencing within oneself what actually belongs to other perceived persons or objects" (1947, p. 496). When we sympathize, we are preoccupied with the assumed duality or the parallel between our own feelings and the feelings of others. We are not concerned so much with the objective reality and character of the other person's situation as with an analogy between him and ourselves. The analogy pre-empts our attention. The understanding of the other person is not our objective.

This distinction is important. Unless it is sharply made, it will be difficult to appreciate empathy as a professional tool in the arts and sciences. Practitioners of empathy are committed to objective knowledge of other personalities. If we use our own feelings, it is for the purpose of learning more about what actually belongs to the other person. But we do not exercise our own feelings to gratify our needs. When we sympathize, we are aware of our own state of mind and much of our attention is still devoted to our own needs. When we empathize we cannot fully escape our own needs but we discipline ourselves to use our own feelings as instruments of cognition. This is particularly true of the artist, the scientist, and the psychotherapist.

When we have sympathetic feelings in our encounters with others, we become even more sharply aware of ourselves. Our self-consciousness is intensified. "On hearing my brother give a cry of pain," said Miguel De Unamuno, "my own pain awakens and cries in the depth of my own consciousness" (1954, p. 151). Sympathy is reactive. It turns our attention back on ourselves. Sometimes our contact with others agitates us so strongly that we must tie up all our emotional energy in maintaining our own emotional equilibrium. We then have no energy for experiencing freely what the other person is feeling. The empathizer tends to abandon his self-consciousness. He does not feel with the other person as if running along on a parallel track. The sense of similarity is so strong that the two become one—his own identity fuses with the identity of the other. Artists speak of the "annihilation of the subject in the object." There is no longer a distance between the subject and the object, when the subject feels himself into the object in the temporary act of empathy. When we empathize, we lose ourselves in the new identity we have temporarily assumed. When we sympathize, we remain more conscious of our separate identity.

Sympathy has many shortcomings as a cognitive process. Preoccupation with our own feelings blunts our sensitivity to others. When we see the slightest indication of a similarity of feeling between the other person and ourselves, we may imagine that the correspondence between him and ourselves is complete. We are then no longer curious about his feelings because we take for granted that they are identical with our own. We thus project our own feelings on the other person. Having received one or two cues which enable us to establish a link between him and ourselves, we subsequently have no doubt about the accuracy of our estimation of his total situation.

In common usage, empathy like sympathy designates affection and warmth. But even in the popular mind it is associated with perception and understanding. Unless we take care to add the word *understanding*, the term *sympathetic*, standing by itself, will signify a positive feeling but not cognition. When we tell someone we are sympathetic about the loss of a parent he has sustained, we inform him about our own state of mind. We offer our own feelings as a symbol of our regard for him. We are also telling him that we think we understand how he feels, but this, I believe, is secondary. When we see a sleeping child who is completely trusting and peaceful, our feelings of warmth and sympathy are evoked, but we could hardly say that the evocation of such feelings contributes anything to our greater understanding of the child.

Empathic appreciation is illustrated in the report of the mother who described a method of understanding her baby through imaginative or psychological empathy. She put herself in the position of her infant and imagined the experience of someone who had suddenly dropped on a strange planet and was surrounded by giants. Huge faces stared at her and mammoth hands reached down to her. Suppose, the mother explained, that I had never felt water or tasted food or heard laughter and loud voices. Would I not appreciate any effort by my benefactor to caress and reassure me? By making an analogy between the situation of her new baby and her own imagined situation as a sudden visitor to a strange planet, she was able to apprehend the needs of her infant in a way that had never before been possible for her. Her study of books on child psychology had given her an intellectual understanding. Her listening to the advice of other mothers had enlightened her on specific points of infant behavior. But she could not grasp the infant's personality and its own world in its completeness until she tried the method of empathy.

When we empathize we take on the personality of another person and try out his experiences. We do not presume, as in sympathizing, that his personality is already a copy of our own. Thus Downey defines empathy:

Through subtle imitation we assume an alien personality, we become aware of how it feels to behave thus and so, then we read back into the other person our consciousness of what his pattern of behaviour feels like (1929, p. 177).

If empathy is close to sympathy as a process of feeling, it also has something in common with the cognitive processes of intuition and telepathy. These processes participate in a nonrational quality and tend to be primitive, prelogical, and instinctive. Empathy remains distinctive, however, because it calls for a personal involvement and an engagement of the self of the knower. No such involvement of the personality takes place when we have sudden intuitions. It is true that when flashes of insight occur and new linkages are formed in the mind there is no conscious or deliberate intellectual effort involved. But the process is still intellectual. Pieces of information come together and new meanings emerge. Information accrues to the knower. But the self of the knower is only a passive receiver on which bits of data or complete Gestalten are recorded. There is no imaginative or felt activity of one person becoming identified with another. Whatever empathy may share with other nonrational forms of cognition, the process must specify an imaginative or emotional involvement of the self and the object.

The Practitioners of Empathy

We here defer a more detailed inquiry into the origins and components of the empathic skill to survey the professional roles in which empathy is used. We have already considered empathy in a phenomenological way and have noted that it is an everyday experience which promotes communication and offers certain emotional gratifications. Empathy is relevant to the objectives of several sciences and especially to the helping professions. Its practice has been cultivated in depth by counselors and by psychoanalysts in particular.

Who are the professional empathizers in our society? In what social roles is empathy a prerequisite? For the purpose of an overview at this point we note that professional concern with

empathy as a cognitive technique varies with the degree of interest the scientist or practitioner has in the inner experiences of his
subjects or his clients. The greater the need for empathic knowledge the more likely is the investigator to involve himself empathically with the individual who is the focus of his professional
attention.

Among researchers in the pure sciences we would expect the
psychologist to be more concerned with the use of empathy than
the zoologist. For the geologist or the physicist, empathy would
be irrelevant except for such curiosity as the scientist might have
concerning his colleagues and the processes by which they se-
lected certain problems and worked through to certain conclusions. The actual material with which such scientists work
obviously makes no demands on their empathic powers. In the
applied science of medicine, we observe that the surgeon has
less need of empathy than does the pediatrician. The anaesthetist,
in turn, having even less contact with the conscious patient and
less responsibility for his psychic states, has less need to cultivate
empathy than does the surgeon. The psychoanalyst, on the other
hand, is faced with a maximum challenge in gaining an appreciation of the total personality of his patient and is deeply involved
in the practice of empathy. Counselors and psychotherapists in
general cultivate the practice of empathy to a degree that is
rare in other professions because they require an intimate appreciation of inner experiences, conflicts, and attitudes. For them
empathy is often a strategic factor in making diagnoses, and it is
often decisive in the establishment of a helping relationship.

There is a continuum of involvement, ranging from certain
sciences or professions, where empathic knowledge is only remotely relevant—like the geological or the mathematical sciences
—to others, like teaching, nursing, or the ministry, where the expectations of empathic involvement are distinctively stronger.
We would assume that the anthropologist would have a respect
for empathic methods because of his professional concern with
studying cultures from the inside. Those who work in the creative and the performing arts like poets, playwrights, and actors
can be presumed to have an uncommon interest in empathic processes. Among the practitioners, the counselors and therapists are

probably the most deliberate and the most disciplined users of empathy. They use it deliberately and ingeniously and are the most likely to be able to analyze and interpret its advantages as a refined and sophisticated technique.

Counselors and therapists have found it necessary to cultivate their empathic powers because of the cognitive difficulties they face and because they recognize that discipline and training are necessary if they are to avoid possible errors in empathizing. They need to be alert to every possible channel for making fuller human contact. As specialists in human relations, they also try to evoke confidence in their clients and patients so that private feelings may be revealed more easily. Like the clergy they seek to establish empathic relationships which are marked by unusual rapport and understanding.

We turn to some statements by psychotherapists in order to appreciate both the nature and the function of empathy in professional practice. These are formulations made by psychoanalytic specialists, but the methods of empathizing they describe are applicable to other helping professions as well. The relevance of such empathic techniques is not restricted to those practitioners who concentrate on probing the unconscious or on long-term treatment of deeply disturbed patients. For those whose interest in empathy is more academic, such descriptions provide a helpful clarification of a process of communication.

According to Robert Fliess, the skill of the therapist depends

essentially on his ability to put himself in the latter's place, to step into his shoes, and to obtain in this way an inside knowledge that is almost first-hand. The common name for such a procedure is "empathy"; and we, as a suitable name for it in our own nomenclature, should like to suggest calling it trial identification (1942, p. 212).

Maurice Levine characterizes the "empathic" element in interviewing a "process essentially of limited and temporary identification with the patient." The therapist asks himself, "How would I feel under the same circumstances. If I were in his shoes and behaved in that way, how might I really be feeling?" (1961, p. 208). Dr. Levine believes that empathy, if handled correctly, leads to a type of "immediate comprehension of the patient's problems that in many ways is superior to the intellectual variety of understanding."

Why the Study of Man Requires Empathic Methods

The part that empathy plays in the actual care and treatment of the client will be discussed in a later chapter. Here we are concerned more broadly with a research technique. The counselor or therapist is only one of many practitioners of empathic skills who are persuaded that they must supplement the so-called scientific and objective methods of study with the more empathic and subjective processes. The artist, too, finds empathy useful. It helps him to express and capture in the art form that which he has come to understand about the inner nature of man. Are there rational and objective reasons for believing that the study of man cannot be accomplished by the use of logic alone? Why must the student of human personalities become empathically involved with his subjects? Why must we give up our dependence on reason, the technique for learning in which we have had the most training and which we ordinarily believe is the most objective, scientific, and reliable research tool that we have?

An answer to this question was suggested by the psycho-analysts previously quoted. Fliess, Levine, and others recommend the use of empathy because this technique leads to "inside knowledge that is almost first-hand" and provides an "immediate comprehension" that in some respects may be superior even to intellectual understanding. If we study human personality logically and intellectually, an immediate and direct grasp of the inner core of the person is likely to elude us. We are unable to appreciate the subtleties and nuances of his emotions. We fail to comprehend him as a human being. Logic or abstract thinking disappoints us if we rely on it exclusively to give us insight into the emotional life. The emotions are too complex and too varied. Logic also disappoints us if we intend to study a particular human personality in its uniqueness and individuality. Reason is most useful when we assign the individual to a category. It falls wide of the mark when we aim to understand a man not in terms of his similarities with others but in terms of his own personal and private characteristics.

The case for empathy rests on the fact that however similar human beings may be, there is something distinctive and unique about each. If our goal is to understand what is individual and distinctive in a person we must use empathic methods. Each individual requires a meticulous personal investigation. The insights we have gained from the study of A, B, and C are helpful when we come to study D, but they cannot be relied upon completely. We must make a fresh effort and avoid pigeonholing subject D in familiar categories. The categories we already have and the general information we already possess are useful as guidelines, but they cannot take the place of the independent and completely new study necessary each time we confront a different person. If we want to understand the moods and needs of Mr. Harry Smith, we must empathize with him as the specific and independent personality that he actually is. There is something about Harry Smith, as about every human being, that defies classification.

Were we to think for a moment about Mr. Smith, we would soon find ourselves using such labels as elder in his church, troubled father of two restless teen-agers, overworked grocer, Democrat, or heart case. If we were trying to do a medical diagnosis of Mr. Smith, we might collect clinical data about him that would lead us to classify him as a case of hypertension or of anxiety neurosis. This nomenclature is useful as far as it goes. It alerts us to certain facts and trends in Mr. Smith's illness. But it provides us with only a clue or a guideline if we are concerned with Mr. Smith as a personality. We would have to do much more than classify and interpret certain symptoms in order to gain insight into Mr. Smith's style of living or to appreciate what meaning his body has for him, how he views himself as a father, or what conflicts drive him to overwork.

When we use our reason, we rely on abstractions, laws, and names. We are impatient with the unit or the particular that we cannot manage or control. When we analyze we seek to place each fragment of reality into some intellectual category. We move as quickly as possible from the specific to the universal and from the actual to the conceptual. No matter how brilliant our categorization might be, Mr. Smith would still be standing before us, an object but not a person, a symbol of mankind but not a living, dynamic world in himself. He could neither be cut to the size of our categories nor be caught in the net of our concepts. Our intellect, as Henri Bergson wrote, "is characterized by a natural inability to comprehend life" (1911a, p. 165).

The very tools of logic are verbal abstractions. When we use such tools we cannot avoid stereotyping. When we try to understand a new phenomenon logically, we cannot help but classify it under one kind of law or in one class of objects. The mind is an abstracting instrument. It strips away what is unique and leaves only the universal. We are sure to fail if we approach the human personality only in terms of such universals or stereotypes. It is not only because abstract knowledge is not vivid or first-hand. We would fail if we relied on labels and names simply because no repertory of names could be large enough to emcompass all the shades and varieties of emotions and attitudes in the personality.

There are basic emotions which are universal like love and fear or common emotional experiences like grief or excitement. But the varieties and nuances of these emotions are fantastically great. We have names for the more gross affective states, but we have far too few to encompass the more delicate and subtle. We are baffled when we try to find words that come anywhere near "matching the delicate distinctions of affective response of which men are capable" (Bartlett, 1932, p. 223). If we are poets we may be able to discover or to create a rich verbal imagery that greatly extends the range of our labels. But even the most gifted poet is unable to demonstrate a consistent and comprehensive ability to describe verbally the full intensity of feeling tones that are part of human experience.

Empathy helps us to transcend the limits of our rational powers. When we empathize we are not confined to using the stock of labels or descriptive words at our command. Through our feelings, we sense more of the quality of the feelings of others. Even if we cannot give a name to what the other person is experiencing, to a degree we can experience it ourselves and appreciate it more realistically and accurately.

Even if we found a name for the experience of the other person, our appreciation of that experience would be constricted. As soon as we employ verbal symbols, our knowledge becomes more indirect and less sensitive. When we think logically, our tools are concepts or words rather than experiences. We have already placed a distance between ourselves as subjects and the other persons as objects. "A feeling that is named," wrote Robert Briffault, "is no longer a feeling. It is the presentation of a feeling, a mere cognition" (1921, p. 61). When we understand logically, we miss the immediacy of knowing. In the appreciation of the complexity and mystery of the human personality, there are degrees of concreteness and reality of understanding. When the knower employs his own feeling and does not rely exclusively on concepts that are necessarily abstract and stereotyped, he understands more profoundly. W. J. Bates, the literary historian, distilled the essence of the argument when he described the Romantic and individualistic theme in eighteenth-century English literature:

Feeling transcends what is usually regarded as "reason," not only because it offers a more spontaneous vitality of realization, but also because it is aware of nuances of significance and of interrelationships to which the logical process is impervious (1956, p. 130).

The poets and essayists of eighteenth-century England had been conversant with empathic processes and had recognized them as indispensable to the creative artist. They opposed the Classicist emphasis on reason and its reliance on formal and static concepts. As Romanticists they devoted attention to the individual and to the emotional and subjective sides of his nature. They believed that the sudy of man could not be accomplished by reason un- aided by the emotions of the observer.

Echoes of the Romantic-Classicist conflict continue to reverberate in modern philosophy, art, and science. The arguments for more empathic methods in the humanities and in science have been repeated by existentialist and phenomenological thinkers from Kierkegaard to Martin Buber. For a genuine understanding of the individual in all his uniqueness, such thinkers assert that we the knowers must become involved with the "objects" we study. We can manipulate "objects" with our reason, but if we wish to understand the human character in depth, we must supplement the use of reason with other faculties and must engage our total personalities. The traditional separation of subject from object, the detached and analytic viewpoint, must be rejected. The student of man must draw on his own subjective processes and take the risk of so-called nonrational techniques of communication and apprehension.

A forthright case for the use of empathy was stated by the American sociologist, Charles H. Cooley, in 1926. He distinguished between two kinds of knowledge, spatial or material knowledge and personal or social knowledge. We are endowed with different kinds of equipment appropriate for each task. To master spatial or material knowledge about things, we have instruments of measurement and classification. Our senses of sight and touch and our capacity for reason help us cope with our material when we work in the natural sciences. But we have other senses or sensibilities which help us to understand human behavior and motivation. They consist of dramatic, imaginative, and feeling modes of knowing.

Empathic abilities are more appropriate in the study of persons than of things because we are concerned with appreciating rather than with explaining or analyzing inner experiences. When we explain, we are concerned with problems of origin, with quantities, and with classifications in terms of regularities or laws. Explaining consists of an exercise in logic. Understanding, on the other hand, involves an appreciation of qualities. When we understand another person, we know him as a totality. We realize who and what he is as he experiences himself. We want to comprehend the other person's actual experience. This cannot be achieved by invoking more general laws of cause and effect or by "adding up arithmetically the pieces of information which the patient presents you with" (Lumeij, 1957, p. 19). In the study of persons and their inner experiences and qualities, we have a research aim that is different but fully as respectable as other research aims that are concerned with statistics and laws.

Positivistic scientists contain or suppress the sensitivities and feelings that might contaminate the field of research. Others who are equally concerned with truth exploit their feelings in the service of science and objective knowledge. Activity within the psyche of the researcher provides data that are otherwise unattainable.

Any scientific judgment of empathy as a cognitive technique must take into consideration the fact that the problems to be solved are of such complexity and such subtlety that ordinary standards of measurement are simply not relevant. The police investigator may use a lie detector to get some objectively measurable index of certain gross emotional changes in his subject. He and his associates can read the ups and downs on the blood pressure chart and draw certain general inferences. The process is scientific in so far as pointer readings are made and are available for comparative judgment by a group of observers. Far less scientific are the interpretations made of these readings. However satisfying the use of instruments and machines may be, it is doubtful that they would lead to an understanding in depth of the personality of the accused. The empathic researcher finds such a presumably scientific procedure to be deficient and aims at a more penetrating, comprehensive, and hence more scientific study of personality. He does not rely on standardized scientific techniques nor is he content with measurable and often superficial research data. It is true that some projective techniques in psychological testing are based on a standard set of symbols. A variety of subjects set down their associations to a common set of ink blots or pictures. In such forms of research there is relatively little empathic communication between the tester and the particular subject. Yet such testing does involve some empathic responses on the part of the investigator. He cannot score the responses automatically by consulting his catalogue of responses. He must use the data of other researchers and employ some of the established categories. But in the interpretation of the client's associations, the tester must put himself into the position of the client and feel with him as he tries to comprehend the emotional forces in the subject that evoked such responses.

The human material with which the therapist or the social

scientist deals cannot be converted into a formula. A personality
we presume to be *sui generis* in many ways cannot be reduced to
a statistic or a category. Max Weber pointed out that when we
are concerned with the empathic understanding of psychological
and intellectual phenomena, we are tackling "a problem of a
specifically different type from those which the schemes of the
exact natural sciences in general can or seek to solve" (1949, p.
74).

How Scientific Is Empathic Knowledge?

The empathic researcher is aware of the fact that even his
methods may not lead to the fullest appreciation of the inner
feelings of another person. His efforts fall short because some
depths and nuances of human experience remain permanently out
of the reach of either his intellect or his feelings. If he is a psychoanalyst and spends many years communicating with a single
patient, he knows that extensive as his knowledge of the patient
may be, it is still incomplete. He may not fully understand the
patient's past and he is likely to miss part of the meaning that
the patient's ever changing present may have for him. Even if the
empathizer does not accept Bergson's judgment that "our souls
are impenetrable to one another," he recognizes the limitations of
human understanding (1911b, p. 166). Moved by scientific
curiosity as well as by therapeutic ambitions, he will push as far
as he can to the outward limits of human communication and in
that effort he finds that empathy combined with intellectual
analysis takes him farther than reason alone.

Even though the practitioner of empathy takes pains to balance
his use of subjective methods with the more conventional methods
of rational analysis and dispassionate judgment, his status as a
scientist is often challenged. It is true that errors can be made in
the use of empathy. There can be deficiencies and distortions in
empathy as there can be errors in analyzing and in drawing
inferences. The empathizer is often the target of sharp criticism
because he dares to use methods that are still considered untested

and invalid by those who adhere to more conventional methods of pursuing science.

Some researchers who use empathic methods are prone to failure in attempting to feel their way into the situation of others. They are defective in role-taking. Research in social psychology reveals that errors in empathy are made by individuals who tend to project, who lack insight, who are ethnocentric, and who are hypochondriacal. Even those who are presumed to be more mature emotionally find that their empathizing has been unreliable and unrealistic. Failures in empathic communication on the part of counselors are not uncommon. Professional scholars who use empathy fall into error through a process which Gottschalk called "vicarious egocentricism." The historical writer becomes vulnerable when he identifies with a figure so strongly that he makes entirely too much of the role played by this figure in the events of his era.

That skill and talent are essential in the professional use of empathy is obvious. That empathic knowledge must be checked and evaluated whenever possible is also true. The potentiality for error is in itself, however, no argument against the validity of the empathic method.

Usual methods of scientific validation cannot always be applied to the results achieved by empathic methods. We say that a particular solution to a problem is scientifically true when there is agreement among different students about its validity. How could we attempt to reach this kind of consensus when we deal with psychological matters involving so many subjective variables? Often it does happen that different interviewers making an empathic study of the same client will concur in appreciating the same features of the client's inner experience. To this extent the scientific criterion of validity might be said to have been complied with successfully. But other phases of understanding are not so easily tested. In the first place, one member of the team of interviewers might penetrate to certain phases of the client's personality that had been missed by the others. Another interviewer may have had a greater native or trained capacity for empathy. The client is a variable also. He may have responded more openly and revealed more of himself to a particular therapist because of some unpredictable and uncontrollable element in his personal reaction to the personality of that therapist. The data that came to this interviewer, perhaps fortuitously, were not available to his colleagues and hence could not be checked by them. Second, empathic understanding is something that is experienced by the empathizer. He is not completely able to symbolize with words his feeling about the client. When he begins to describe what he feels *after* empathizing with the client, he has already moved from intense feeling to a level of abstraction. He can convey only part of his empathic knowledge. What he cannot convey in words cannot be fully communicated to his colleagues. They, in turn, have no standard criteria for judging whether they can accept his data.

We have pressed the problem of scientific verification to a logical extreme in order to demonstrate certain insoluble problems in evaluating empathic research. Apart from such theorizing, we can say that, relatively speaking, a degree of consensus exists among different therapists in their empathic understanding of a given client. Certain nuances of understanding that one therapist might achieve and that another might miss may also be said to be realistic and objective, even though they cannot be evaluated by the method of agreement among authorities.

The client often confirms the accuracy of the therapist's understanding. He may feel that his therapist appreciates him from the inside. If he has had more than one therapist, he may assess therapist A as being more (or less) empathic than therapist B. Here again we would be hard put to measure the client's responses objectively. The client's feeling about his therapist would be internal and subjective. He would be unable to translate his feelings into words with complete faithfulness. Therapists and clients often communicate in nonverbal or empathic ways. The therapist might "sense" that he is intimately in touch with his client. But this kind of impression is a matter of inner sensitivity not easily crystallized in words and therefore difficult to verify.

Agreement among specialists is one criterion of scientific validity. The ability of the researcher to make successful predictions is another. The kind of knowledge the empathizer attains frequently enables him to predict the responses of his client.

When he is able to do this, his hunches about the client become more scientifically reputable. But the criterion of predictability cannot be applied too rigorously in the study of personality. Human nature is so elusive and so dynamic that a therapist can be said to have valid knowledge of the feelings of his client at a particular time without being able to predict what his client will feel in a new combination of circumstances and a new environment. In the last analysis, the most important index to the validity of his empathic understanding is the response of the client, who indicates, either verbally or nonverbally, that he feels he is understood. If the client has this feeling about his therapist as a continuous experience, the latter can be reasonably sure that his empathy has been accurate.

Submitting the subjective responses of the client as evidence of the validity of the therapist's knowledge might seem to be a shaky bit of evidence. The client might easily be mistaken. We would use one unknown—the client's empathy into the therapist —to test another unknown—the therapist's empathy into the client. Yet it remains the most valid index we have.

Are We Free to Empathize?

Even if we are not defensive about using empathy, we are not always comfortable in our practice of it. We are not always sure of our competence nor are we always able to shake off a certain reservation about using a technique that seems more typical of the artist than of the scientist. So much seems to depend on the subjective variable. The limits of empathic power are determined by the empathic ability and imagination of the individual practitioner. Most practitioners of empathy in the social sciences and in psychotherapy have been born and bred into a tradition that favored the methods of the natural sciences. The logic and philosophy they studied was based on the Cartesian principle that the subject and the object must be separated. They have been indoctrinated with the principle that science is neutral and detached. Much psychology still favors the empirical and statistical methods of the natural sciences. Clinicians and therapists fight to reverse this stand, but even they are not completely emancipated from the cultural taboo on subjective methods.

We seek to control our materials and to control our own responses. It is natural that empathy, which allows for the play of the imagination and the evocation of feeling, should appear to be regressive. When we empathize, we permit spontaneous activities to emerge. Once they are set in motion, some of our responses are spontaneous and involuntary. We seem more like the playful child than the self-disciplined and mature adult. We need not view such childlike activity as inappropriate or dysfunctional. It is a regression "which serves the ego," a momentary indulgence in fantasy that ultimately gives us a more accurate understanding of reality. If we want to empathize we must take the risk of relaxing our self-control, giving up temporarily our carefully cultivated habits of alert observation, and surrendering to nonrational processes. Even the most experienced therapists find it difficult to follow Freud's recommendations about suspending attention and avoiding the construction of conscious expectations. We do not relish the state of being off guard that often goes with any relaxation of attention. Even though we are able to terminate our empathic response, we are engaged by it for the moment and we are subject to unpredictable and disturbing feelings. Abstractions and concepts are remote from us and threaten us less than people and the feelings that connect us with them.

We feel more secure when we can deal with instruments or with procedures that are standardized. We can be sure of our adequacy in the use of the slide rule. Its symbols are universally recognized. Once we become proficient in its use, we know that we have a reliable instrument at our command. Even the procedures of philosophic analysis, however abstract, seem more tangible than the elusive and fluctuating processes of empathy. We can check our intellectual operations against categories of thought and laws of evidence that are universally recognized. But empathy offers us less reliable checkpoints. We must deal with two subjective variables: first, our own personality and second, the personality of the individual we wish to understand. It is hard to isolate the constants in empathic activity. We have to find our way again each time we study a different person. Even then our course is subject to change because the client with whom we empathize is far from static.

Anyone who empathizes must be able to trust his own feelings and his instincts. Because we have been trained in rationalistic methods and because we have been indoctrinated with a prejudice that emotions are disorganizing, we are ill-prepared for a plunge into subjective experiences as part of our research.

We are also inhibited in using empathy because we distrust our ability to regain objectivity once we permit our feelings to become involved. If we open the lid on the Pandora's box of inner excitement, will we be able to snap it shut again? Our own problems, those that we have not solved or have not adequately repressed, may be stirred up again. We are not comfortable with the contagion of emotional stimulation. We tend to hold on to the kind of emotional controls we have, and to do this we keep high the barriers between our clients and ourselves. If we need our own energies to maintain a personal *status quo*, we shall not be free to divert any of them to experiment with other reactions.

Some of our inhibition comes from professional as well as personal concerns. If we empathize or make a trial identification, we may not be able to extricate ourselves from the net of feeling. The anthropologist may overidentify with the careers of the natives he studies and disqualify himself for dispassionate reporting of scientific data. An extreme case of this was Frank Cushing whose identification with the Pueblo Indians turned out to be permanent. He joined the tribe!

The practitioner of empathy must obviously be prepared to resist conforming to a highly rationalistic culture. He must be willing to experiment with different roles in his imagination. Finally, he must be both willing and competent to balance his identifications or empathic acts with a skill for detaching himself and for withdrawing for the purpose of objective assessment. The gains from empathic understanding make both the effort and the risk worthwhile.

II

THE PENDULUM BETWEEN
EMPATHY AND OBJECTIVITY

EMPATHY CONSISTS of feeling. It involves the inner experience of feeling oneself to be similar to or nearly identical with the other person. There is an important distinction between simple empathy and the use of empathy as a technical and specialized cognitive technique.

Both simple or raw empathy and empathy as the tool of the scientist are capable of yielding objective information not attainable through ordinary rational and intellectual techniques. When empathy is used in a professional way, it becomes more consistently effective, more versatile, and more penetrating. With discipline, empathy or "empathic understanding" becomes a fully reputable scientific technique. What distinguishes simple empathy from the more sophisticated process of empathic understanding is the combination of subjective and critical processes. As a re-

26

fined scientific technique, used by social scientists and by members of the helping professions, empathy calls for a pendulum-like action, alternating between subjective involvement and objective detachment.

The distinction between raw and sophisticated empathy would be easier to grasp if we could point to a dramatic term that would epitomize the more disciplined process. We have no nomenclature to help us distinguish sharply between the empathy of everyman and the empathy of the artist, of the anthropologist, or of the psychotherapist. Theodor Reik used the term "listening with the third ear." For lack of a better term, we shall refer to the disciplined, scientific use of empathy as a process of "empathic understanding," implying a technical process that includes both subjective feeling and objective analysis. The specifically empathic element in this process could be rendered as "taking the role of the other" in sociologic terms, as "feeling into" in the language of aesthetics, and as "trial identification" in the professional terminology used in psychoanalysis.

It should be clear that those who use empathy in a disciplined way are far from being partisans of the irrational or enemies of reason. They do not aim to "play down the mind and to play up the emotions." They do not deserve the judgment made by Hegel of those who communicate only by way of feeling-states —"the condition of mere animals." The poet Stefan Zweig has well expressed the harmonious use of subjective and objective methods in Freud's method of psychological investigation: "Thus he was actively entering into an alien personality while simultaneously contemplating it from without with the dispassionate gaze of the psychological diagnostician" (1962, p. 269).

Intimations of Empathy

The modern researcher or psychotherapist puts to scientific use a certain appreciation of empathy that has long been familiar in the arts and the humanities. When he involves himself, participating inwardly in the experiences of others and using his sense of likeness or identity with them as a cognitive technique,

he employs a principle of empathy that has been intuitively and
spontaneously comprehended outside of science. Some parallels
or intimations of empathic understanding are worth noting as
part of our larger appreciation of empathy as a phenomenon both
in and out of science.

The basic principle that we comprehend what we resemble
has long been appreciated in the creative arts, religious poetry, as
well as historical scholarship. Whether the artist and the poet
grasp the place of this psychological fact in a theory of cognition
is not an issue. They use it in their evocation and interpretation
of human emotions. Those who work professionally with people
make a somewhat self-conscious effort to induce within themselves some feeling of identity with them. To the artist it comes
naturally. He must lose himself in his work so that subject and
object become one. The act of becoming similar or identical
gives him a sharpness and directness of experience which can
then be captured and preserved in objective forms through the
symbols of art.

The novelist or poet who is artistically effective has alternated
between the intense subjective experience of identifying and the
more objective role of communicating this experience in a tangible or objective form. Those who appreciate the artistic or
literary creation of others engage in empathy as well. They
identify with the creative artist himself and "live over again" the
emotions he experienced in at least one phase of the original
creative process. When they examine a portrait or a poem criti-
cally, they withdraw from the subjective feeling of union with
the artist or with his creations and then, from a distance, evaluate
and compare dispassionately.

The artist or the poet has the power to resemble the individuals, real or imaginary, he wishes to describe in art forms.
He assumes the feelings of the character he draws and becomes
for a moment the very person whom he portrays. Shakespeare
is said to have had a rare talent for identification. According to
William Hazlitt, the bard was

nothing in himself; but he was all that others were, or that they
could become. He not only had in himself the germs of every faculty
and feeling, but he could follow them by anticipation, intuitively, into

all their conceivable ramifications, through every change of fortune, or conflict of passion, or turn of thought. . . . He had only to think of anything in order to become that thing, with all the circumstances belonging to it (Bates, 1956, p. 143).

Balzac believed that he had such a talent. He spoke of powers of intuitive observation which gave him the faculty for living the life of the individual portrayed in his novel. He could substitute himself for his character. Balzac, like Shakespeare and other artists with rich empathic endowments, had the capacity for entering totally into his subject so that his own identity, for a time, was almost completely obliterated.

D. T. Suzuki tells a story dramatizing the principle that the artist must resemble the object he wishes to paint. An abbot of a monastery wanted to have the ceiling painted with a dragon and commissioned a painter to undertake the assignment. The painter was somewhat reluctant to paint a dragon because he had never seen one. The abbot then urged him to become one and then paint it. The prescription for the artist was to concentrate so intensely on being a dragon that he would ultimately feel that he had assumed the identity of such a creature. The resemblance between the artist and his subject must be so close, Suzuki concluded, that "the artist must get into the thing and feel it inwardly and live its life himself" (1960, p. 13).

In writing *The Magic Mountain*, Thomas Mann must have become the young hero Hans Castorp, experiencing with him the day by day life in a mountaintop sanitarium. A dramatic actor immerses himself in a number of different roles and by a talent for combining subjective experience with the self-discipline of the stage is able to evoke similar feelings among members of the audience. In portraying Hamlet, Sir John Gielgud engages in a number of feats of empathy. He feels himself into the mind of the author and becomes Shakespeare at one point. He identifies with the imaginary character that the playwright had evoked out of his own creative powers. At the same time, Gielgud must take the position of members of the audience so that he can feel their mood as intensely as if he were spectator instead of actor. His sense of timing reflects his awareness of their responses. He strives to resemble a number of people, while simultaneously

retaining his own sense of identity as professional actor and
sensitive human being.

The art of the biographer often depends on the author's
ability to evoke within himself the milieu and the experience of
the subject of his study. An incident in the career of Catherine
Drinker Bowen makes persuasively clear the kind of special insight that is gained when the writer is able to take up the position of her subject. In one sense it might be objected that Mrs.
Bowen was physically experiencing an event, but the feeling and
the sweep of the imagination justify our classifying this incident
as typical of imaginative empathy. Trying to gather material for
her study of Oliver Wendell Holmes, Mrs. Bowen decided to
visit the paternal home and learn more about Holmes' father.
While visiting Dr. Holmes' room, she took note of a mirror that
was hung quite low on the back of a door. She observed that
when she faced the mirror she could see no higher than her own
shoulders and she thought it odd for a mirror to have been kept in
such a position. She learned that the glass had been set quite
far down in order that it could be useful to Dr. Holmes. Mrs.
Bowen had known that Dr. Holmes was a short man but the
significance of this fact had previously escaped her. When she
re-experienced the position once occupied by Dr. Holmes, she
was able to understand him from within. She made herself resemble the good doctor by literally standing in the position he
had once occupied. As a biographer she then gained an altogether
new insight into the meaning that Dr. Holmes' shortness of
stature must have had for him. "Yet until I saw the mirror, it
was not borne in upon me fully what the life and outlook of so
small a man must be. No wonder the Doctor was so cocky and
strutted a bit. A man had to, whose face fitted into that low-
slung piece of glass" (Bowen, 1959, p. 57).

Religious literature affords us a number of examples of the
principle that we comprehend those whom we resemble. Taken
literally, these sources refer to the concrete and actual experiencing of what others experience. Moses, living as an Egyptian
prince, came to understand the slave people of Israel when he
made himself similar to them by participating in their suffering.
Jesus, too, walked among the common people and by his identi-

fication with them came to comprehend their needs. Taken more figuratively, many of the themes in the religious traditions imply a recognition of the principle of imaginative projection into the situation of the other person. A Jewish legend explains the way in which God came to comprehend the people. He made Himself like them. The Hebrew root *shavah* means to make equal or make identical with. The term is applied to God's activity of going into exile with Israel. He becomes a partner in their suffering. The dramatic account of God's empathy for man was very likely intended as an admonition to mortals to sharpen their own sensitivities by imagining themselves to be in the position of others (Katz, 1959).

The principle of loving thy neighbor as thyself (Leviticus 19:18) implies an *as-if* or empathic activity. One relates to his neighbor as if he were his neighbor himself. The well-known rabbinic maxim "do not judge your fellow until you have come into his place" (Mishnah Avoth 2:5) states the empathic principle explicitly. The Hasidim, a mystic group in Judaism which arose in the early modern period, reported the activities of the saintly teachers who made themselves similar to the common people by descending from the ladder of holiness and involving themselves in the lives of others. In Dresner's translation of a hasidic source, "one who intends to raise his friend from the mire and refuse, must himself go down to that mire and refuse, in order to bring him up" (1960, p. 180). To avoid being swamped by the troubles of the person, the religious teacher was reminded to tie a rope around himself before making a descent. The rope was the symbolic rope of faith and the "descent" an imaginative, or *as-if*, activity. The religious leaders known as Tzaddikim were expected to understand their followers because they shared the same impulses and the potentialities for the same experiences. They also could assume the specific role of their people. We find a parable of empathy in the hasidic story of the lost prince who is finally returned to his father. A king had sent a number of his nobles to search for the prince. Everyone failed to find the prince until one of the nobles took the step of making himself resemble one of the common people with whom the prince was keeping company. Putting on the kind of clothing worn by the villagers and assuming their identity, this man ultimately was able to find something in common with the prince and, by communicating with him as a member of his group, he was able to persuade the prince to return to his father (Dresner, 1960, pp. 177 ff.). The central drama of Christianity treated the same theme. In Christian dogma, God took the form of man. Dramatized in the person of Jesus who walked among men, the divine message was communicated more directly and intimately and salvation was made more comprehensible. The theme of empathic identification is prominent in religious literature, in ceremony, and in liturgy. With instinctive wisdom, religious seers endorsed empathy as an ethical discipline, recognizing the fact that altruistic feelings are generated in empathic role-taking.

Comprehending Whom We Resemble

Before attempting to interpret the modern and scientific technique of empathic understanding, it is necessary to clarify the logical basis for the principle that we comprehend those whom we resemble. The sociologist Ferdinand Tönnies noted this correlation when he observed that "Understanding is more probable when the constitution, the experience, the character, and the intellectual attitude of two people are similar" (1940, p. 54).

Some recent empirical research by Milton Rokeach has underscored the fact that empathic similarity is not just a function of membership in the same religious or ethnic group. Empathy among individuals who hold the same beliefs may be even stronger than among those bound by ties of race or cultural group. What is essential for our discussion is that empathy follows similarity, whatever the source of such likeness. We must still ask why it is that similarity between ourselves and others helps us to apprehend the experience of others more completely and more intimately. What is the rationale for the "trial identification" that the researcher or psychotherapist makes with his subject or client? Logic affords us the outline of an answer. Sociology provides us with another clue.

According to the logic of effective communication, we understand each other's messages when the words, symbols, and gestures have the same meaning for each partner in the dialogue. Symbols held in common evoke a common response. We learn through social experience and through observing the consequences of the messages we send that a given symbol or abstraction has the same meaning or value for ourselves and for others. If the code were not shared by both parties to the communication, the transmission of meaning would be blocked. We would use the same words but speak quite different languages. When the signals produce similar or roughly identical effects, we are confident that we are "in touch." A two-way passage has been opened.

Members of closely allied groups share a sense of mutuality and solidarity in addition to possessing a set of verbal symbols in common. They have coexperienced the same events and they participate in a common destiny. One member understands the other because he has personally lived through the same life situation.

When we empathize in everyday experiences, we enjoy a sense of membership in the same group and participate in communications that are based on a common understanding of verbal symbols. In empathic understanding the practitioner not only appreciates symbols in the way his subject does—he becomes the subject by making a trial identification. The resemblance of minds is extended to include a resemblance of emotional states. The empathizer already shares many common human experiences and emotions with the subject. In the act of empathy, the feeling he already shares is augmented by the imaginative activity, which enables him to share more closely and more personally. The involvement of his self in the self of the other becomes a means of establishing a stronger feeling of identity. In the terms of the sociologist, we reduce social distance when we take the role of the other. The more closely we can approximate the position of the other person, the more his "presence" becomes real and immediate. We experience it as though it were our own.

Even when we engage in formal and intellectual communication, we try to achieve a similarity of meaning. When we try to understand the ideas of another person, we are obliged in part to *stand under* him and to determine what the words and concepts mean when they are received by the other person. In psychological understanding where we are interested in emotional realities and internal psychic states, we *stand under* the situation of the other person more comprehensively and more intensely. We try to make ourselves similar to the total personality and include within ourselves his emotions and sentiments as well as his intellectual assumptions and the questions that may be implicit in his mind.

In empathic understanding the similarity is imaginative. The empathizer may have had comparable experiences, but he does not experience actual events in common with his subject nor does he engage in concrete activity in the form of a "trial experience." He does not imitate the subject overtly like the Egyptian millionaire who was reported to have acted out his empathy for deprived countrymen by actually living the life of the poor, putting on sackcloth, walking around as a barefoot beggar, and calling out for alms on the same street corners where earlier in the day he had distributed charity to the indigent. It was a means of becoming as nearly identical as possible; it gave him a thrill and made him feel compassion for the poor (*New York Times*, Nov. 13, 1960, p. 15).

Martin Buber has suggested that we can experience something in common with another person and then jump over to his side, as it were, and re-experience the event from the position of the other person. He gives the example of a caress between a man and a woman. The man might touch the skin of his companion in a gesture that would be tangibly felt by both individuals. He could then experience the other side by imagining what it would be like to be the person who is being caressed. In this interpretation one not only includes the experience of another person but also participates in the experience himself. When we speak of empathic understanding, we *exclude* the actual and overt experience of something in the present. The therapist and the patient do not actually experience the same specific event. The original experience belongs to the other person. The therapist becomes similar because he experiences something from the side of the other person without having participated in the original experience with the patient himself.

The empathizer does not set out to accumulate actual life experiences that will help him empathize with a specific client. It was said of the late Ernest Hemingway that he traveled great distances and risked personal danger soldiering and hunting. He cultivated adventure, and when he came to write his novels, he was able to describe the moments of drama in the lives of his heroes with great vividness. His artistic virtuosity depended on actual experience as well as on rich powers of imagination. Stephen Crane, on the other hand, wrote with rare intensity and dramatic impact about the experience of the soldier without ever having participated in real combat. He had prodigious empathic abilities. In the case of the researcher or therapist using empathy professionally, actual experiences are helpful but not indispensable. He may have had experiences which have given him a sense of likeness with his subject, but such overt experience, either in the past or in the present concurrent with the other person, is not always a prerequisite for effective empathy.

In an empathic relationship we establish two kinds of groups. One is the actual face-to-face meeting between the therapist and his patient. This is a professional meeting or group in which two social roles are involved, the role of the professional and the role of the subject. To some degree there is natural empathy between the members of such a newly formed dyadic group. The professional is never completely bound up in his own role because he also meets his patient as a human being, a father, a member of the same age group, or perhaps of the same religion, and the same socio-economic status. He may very well have personal feelings regarding his client that are natural and realistic.

In addition to actual and overt relationships, the professional and the personal, a second group comes into being. This consists of an *imaginary in-group,* in which the empathizer is both himself and the individual with whom he briefly and provisionally makes an identification. This in-group experience provides the raw material for the empathic insight the practitioner hopes to gain. He hopes to achieve an imaginary or secondary empathy but he cannot induce so subjective a process at will. It is not a matter of incantation. Instinctive capacities for empathy must become active of their own accord. The response of the therapist

is below the level of full awareness. He avoids interfering with
the sense of inner imitation. While he cannot get ready or set
for the experience, he does try to suspend judgment and to relax
some of the self-control which is part of his professional discipline. In another phase of empathic understanding he concen-
trates more deliberately and tries to focus his critical attention
on the meaning of the sense of likeness he has experienced. In
the shuttle-like process of empathic understanding, the empathizer alternates between his actual role as a professional and an
inner role in which he becomes nearly identical with the subject.
There are plays within plays and the fact that actual social
experience with the subject takes place concurrently with
fantasied activity within the empathizer makes the process difficult to appreciate. Responses both actual and fantasied are experienced on a number of different levels all at the same time.
It is not only the practitioner of empathy who senses likeness
to the other person and is projected into the other person's
identity through empathy. The process is often mutual. What
distinguishes the professional empathizer from his subject, with
respect to the empathic factor, is his awareness of the cognitive
value of achieving such likeness and his disciplined use of critical
analysis. As a professional, too, he is likely to be gifted with a
greater than average potential for making identifications and is
surely trained to avoid over- and underidentifying.

Empathic Understanding and the Anthropologist

A cultural anthropologist who has written briefly but in-
sightfully about the process of empathic understanding was the
late Robert Redfield, a scientist by profession and a poet by
avocation.

Redfield's description of the empathic methods of the anthropologist contains the *caveat* that the scientist must come to resemble the native he intends to understand. It is not just a
question of making a field trip to a particular village, of collecting
artifacts, photographs, and interviews. These research practices
are preliminary. Like Goethe, who recommended a visit to the

land of the poet whose lines we wish to understand, the anthropologist travels to the locale of the alien culture. But he does more than become a participant observer, as Redfield was careful to point out. He must assume the identity of an alien personality. The overt and empirical activities of watching a ritual dance or sharing the same food and the same dwelling are immensely helpful to the anthropologist, but unless he comes to resemble the native in his own feelings and responses, he misses the inner view.

The investigator has to see the meaning, understand the valuation, and feel the feeling connected with the object or act in the mind of the native.

Ethos requires the investigator to take an inside view that is very deep and very broad. It makes him share the intimacies of conscience and the villager's feelings of shame or guilt (Redfield, 1955, pp. 81, 85).

In trying to achieve a resemblance or identity with the natives, the anthropologist does not listen as an outsider. He accepts their categories and makes their emphasis his own. If he wishes, for example, to understand the strong attachment that the Nuer tribe have to their cattle, it is not sufficient for him to appreciate the economic importance of the animals in the Nuer economy. He must become a member of the tribe and lose himself momentarily in the identity of an individual. He must experience what the cattle mean to the native, quite apart from their economic value or their symbolic function in determining the owner's social status. Such first-hand knowledge requires him to share as much as possible the thoughts and feelings, the lore and the dreams, the associations and the experiences of those whose social life and culture are focused in their role as herdsmen. The data of interviews and of personal observation are valuable in their own right as sources of information. For the empathic anthropologist, these materials help stimulate and evoke an imaginative activity within the scientist, serving as props and cues for an internal drama which absorbs his interest and which makes him abandon for a moment his actual identity, his customary frame of reference, and his native culture. For certain research tasks, the capacity for intense self-absorption is as essential to the researcher as is thoroughness and ingenuity in compiling statistics and observational data.

The anthropologist's scientific work is not complete when he achieves this kind of identification. After getting the "feel" of a culture through "taking the place" of the native, he must then round out the process of empathic understanding by withdrawing and analyzing what he has experienced. Like the artist, he wishes to record his experience in a permanent form that will be accessible to others. He describes what he has found by using verbal symbols. Unlike the artist, who resorts to symbols and allows them to speak for themselves, the scientist attempts to analyze, test, and interpret what he has learned. He does not rely on suggestion. He makes the implicit more explicit. For this goal he must seek to understand and to compare by using his critical intelligence. He must be able to pull out of the state of being possessed and entranced by his subjective experiences. Again, it is Redfield to whom we can look for a reminder of the full swing of empathic cognition, alternating between the subjective and the objective.

If I should come perfectly to share the inside view of the Maya Indian villager, to share all his thoughts and feelings, and yet could state these thoughts and feelings only in his language, in his gesture and act, I should have triumphed over the difficulty of getting the inside view, but of course I should have failed completely as a scholar or scientist (1955, p. 82).

He is not content "with taking a community, apprehended but unanalyzed" into his understanding. Feeling at home in a foreign culture, important as it may be, is only one part of the equation of empathic understanding.

The Model—Oscillating Between Identification and Detachment

Those who use empathy in a professional way aim to combine its advantages with the more familiar advantages of scientific thinking. They speak of an "equilibrium between identification and detachment" or of a "balancing of involvement and dis-engagement."

Some writers have rejected any use of the term "empathy" because they equate it only with subjective experiences. Martin Buber, for example, seems to appreciate the values of empathic understanding but prefers not to use the concept of empathy because it implies the abandonment of self on the part of the observer or the student. Buber describes empathy as a process of "gliding" into the other person through an identification that is physical or motoric. He claims that when we empathize, we lose perspective and cannot evaluate the experience of the other person in terms of a double viewpoint—the experience of the other *and* one's own experience.

Once we move beyond the difficulty in terminology and grasp Buber's ideas we find that much of what he says about nonverbal comprehension and "experiencing the other side" parallels the description of empathic understanding made by psychoanalysts like Theodor Reik or anthropologists like Clyde Kluckhohn and Robert Redfield. Buber prefers the term "inclusion"—*Umfassung*—to empathic understanding when he points to a process of including the experience of the other while retaining our own identity and dealing with our own reactions to the experience. Buber speaks of "concrete imagining" and of "seeing the other." Such activities are cognitively valuable. They make the other person more fully *present*. We watch ourselves from over on the side of the subject. We feel how he must be feeling and at the same time do not lose touch with our own responses to the event. Fenichel has given us a psychoanalytic description of such a process in his definition of empathy:

empathy consists of two acts: (a) an identification with the other person, and (b) an awareness of one's own feelings after the identi-fication, and in this way an awareness of the object's feelings (1945, p. 511).

There are no complete accounts of empathic understanding which might serve as models for detailed analysis. There is no standard procedure because the personal element is inescapable. Even Theodor Reik, who has an unusual gift for psychological explanation, cannot fully account for his own feats of empathy. His personal reports, the most complete available, are fragmentary and suggestive. His empathic powers reflect his idiosyncratic character and personality. He takes us part of the way into the labyrinth of his own unconscious, but he is unable to account for the emergence of each link in the chain of understanding.

Even without complete records of experiences of empathic understanding, we have sufficient data to justify a working formulation of the process. We recognize that a personal variable is inevitably a part of the process and this recognition is itself a fact of scientific value. Some of the broader features of the process can be conceptualized so that our rational and logical grasp of the workings of empathy can be extended.

In actual personal experience no one rigorously follows the specifications of the model of empathic understanding. Spelling out the different steps in merging and detaching makes empathy appear contrived and artificial. Psychological understanding, as Reik observed, comes to us in a roundabout way. It *accrues to us*—we cannot go after it. It emerges when certain conditions are ripe. The stage cannot be set precisely and such instructions as may be given must be loosely followed. Within the self of the empathizer there must be a constant interaction between the conscious and preconscious elements. If we speak of phases of involvement and detachment, we recognize that in actual imaginative and cognitive experience, the interplay is continuous. We cannot predict when, if ever, we will achieve a feeling of identity with the other person nor do we know with any confidence that we can derive objective data from such vicarious feeling. There is an element of a gamble which remains in the experience of even the most skillfully trained researcher or therapist.

A most important variable in empathic understanding is not even mentioned in this model. It is the response of the subject to the practitioner. Any description of empathic activity on the part of the professional presupposes his ability to establish an open and free relationship with his client. There must be an exchange of messages, of cues, both verbal and nonverbal, as well as some elusive sense of *presence* or personal confrontation. The patient must be willing to open himself and reveal his feelings.

The following model presupposes a genuine meeting between the empathizer and his subject.

For the sake of conceptual clarity, we list four phases in the empathic process, following Theodor Reik's outline. They do not necessarily take place in this order. In any case of empathic understanding, however, it is likely that we begin by feeling ourselves into others or coming to resemble them. Identification is therefore listed first in the following series: (1) Identification, (2) Incorporation, (3) Reverberation, and (4) Detachment.

(1) IDENTIFICATION. This is the most characteristic and fundamental activity of the entire sequence. Partly through an instinctive, imitative activity and partly through a relaxation of our conscious controls, we allow ourselves to become absorbed in contemplating the other person and his experiences. It is an indulgence in fantasy which makes us lose our self-awareness. It is essential if we are to become engaged in an experience of others. The capacity for identification can be explained in a number of ways, as we shall observe in Chapter III. Whatever the source of this capacity, it comes into action as part of our response to the other person. If it is only an intellectual effort, made consciously and deliberately, it cannot be said to be genuine identification. When we identify we become engrossed in the personality of another and we lose consciousness of self. Once we are psychically excited in our meeting with others, we let ourselves go in an imitative activity. If we continue to be aware of such imitative impulses, our emotions will not likely be engaged and we will not feel connected to the other person.

There must be different levels of identification. The determining factor is our flexibility in allowing our feelings to become evoked and activated. Ferenczi said that we require a "freedom and uninhibited motility of psychic excitation" (1927, p. 189). We do not conjure up a feeling of identification by vigorously rubbing the Aladdin's lamp of imagination. We become involved almost in spite of ourselves. We are projected into the other person by our own fantasy, response, or feeling. It is not a case of impersonating or imitating because there is no conscious act of taking the role of another. We do not practice or rehearse the role in order to do a masterful imitation. We indulge our own fantasy. Beyond that, the process of identifying must be spontaneous and undisciplined.

We do not project our own feelings on to the other person. The term projection as used in psychoanalysis refers to a defense mechanism in which we attribute our own intentions to others. When we identify empathically, we do not project our attitudes or aims. Our entire consciousness is projected into another person so that the feelings that inhere in others act upon us. Individuals who use projection as a defense against their own anxiety are actually deficient in the capacity to project themselves into the identity of another person.

Since we are primarily concerned with presenting an outline of the process of empathic cognition as it is professionally used, we need not pause at this point to deal with the difficult question of the intensity of our identification. When we ask how complete and how pervasive is the resemblance we enjoy with the other person, we actually ask two questions: first, how broad an area of the experience of another person can be relived or re-experienced by the empathizer? Second, how deeply do we become involved or absorbed in the process? In Chapter V we shall note the contrasting answers given to these questions by Reik and by Buber.

However deep and intense the identification may be, it is of course temporary and subject to interruption by the empathizer. Those who are unable to control their identifications suffer from a serious loss of ego boundaries which indicates pathology. When the practitioner of empathy becomes engaged in a profound act of empathy, he still retains the power to recover his own sense of identity. He may drift with the current, but because he is securely anchored, he is never completely in the power of the tide. The professional is distinguished from the untrained empathizer because he combines the capacity for identifying with a knowledge of the appropriate moment to interrupt the process of letting himself go (Ferenczi, 1927, p. 189).

(2) INCORPORATION. By this term we mean the act of taking the experience of the other person into ourselves. It is hard to

distinguish this phase from the initial act of feeling oneself into the other person. The symbolic meaning of the term "incorporation" will become clearer when we subsequently analyze the empathic skill itself and note that identifying actually means both projecting oneself into the other person and incorporating the other person into ourselves. These are two sides of the same process. When we *identify*, we project our being into others; when we *incorporate*, we introject the other person into ourselves. Both phases are ways in which we come to sense the reality of the experiences of others. One must have a certain sympathy for the psychoanalytic point of view which emphasizes the activities of the unconscious in order to appreciate what is meant by introjection. When we incorporate another's personality we are partly in the grip of an instinct for taking in objects from our environment. What is essential to our understanding of empathy is the idea that it is the experience of another person that we take in rather than an experience of our own which we project onto another. In this phase, we introduce into our own consciousness something that is partly alien and foreign to us. It is another way in which we reduce the social distance between ourselves and others.

So long as we conceive of phases (1) and (2) as reducing social distance, it is actually unimportant whether we think of moving into the position of the other or taking the other person into ourselves. If we press for a distinction it might be this: when we identify, we experience what the other person feels; when we incorporate or take in, we feel his experience as if it were our own. The semantic difficulties—to say nothing of the problems of logical and rationalistic explanation—should not make us miss the fundamental role which these introductory phases play in giving us a greater capacity for apprehending the feelings of others. Both are forms of making a *connection* between the subject and the object.

(3) REVERBERATION. It is not enough for us merely to take in the experience of another or to get the "feel" of what the other person experiences. What does such a feeling signify? Because we have a cognitive interest in the feelings we experience vicari-

ously, we take another step in the sequence, which often leads
to the emergence of deeper understanding. What we have taken
into ourselves now echoes upon some part of our own experience
and awakens a new appreciation.

We do not interrupt our feeling of identity with others. We
allow for an interplay between two sets of experience, the internalized feelings of others and our own experience and fantasy.
It is as though we had a double identity. The two selves, the
internalized other and our own self, interact upon each other.
The *dialectic* between the actual me and the me which is identified with the other person becomes the source of new insight.
Theodor Reik described the process as a vibration in two
rhythms at the same time, a reverberation which yields insights
that appear unpredictably. It is a paradoxical process in which
we are at the same time fully absorbed in the identity of the
other and yet capable of an experience of ourselves as separate
personalities. Part of our self is fused with the identity of the
other. Yet another part of our feeling and thinking is capable of
responding to this experience as the external thing it is.

What is essential in the psychical process going on in the analyst is
—after the stage of observation—that he can vibrate unconsciously
in the rhythm of the other person's impulse and yet be capable of
grasping it as something outside himself and comprehending it
psychologically, sharing the other's experience and yet remaining
above the struggle, *au dessus de la melée* (Reik, 1949, p. 468).

Buber expressed a similar idea when he spoke of a concrete
imagining of the other side without losing sight of one's own
experience. We do not forfeit our own felt activity at the same
time that we live through an experience from the standpoint of
the other person. Both Reik and Buber agree that such a double
experience is possible and are not concerned with the logical
argument that A could not be both A and B at the same time.
They refer to psychological realities which cannot be judged in
the light of formal syllogistic reasoning. Through the fantasy
activity of the human unconscious, a number of selves can be
said to exist simultaneously. The host self—the actual personality

of the empathizer—can embrace the identity of others without at the same time abandoning its own innate identity.

We truly understand that which is part of our own experience, actual or fantasied. The value of the phase called "reverberation" consists in the fact that something familiar to us is evoked by our interaction with the experience of others. Our self-knowledge is therefore sharpened or reawakened. With this deepening of our self-appreciation comes an understanding of what others feel. In trying to account for this advantage, Reik, like other students of empathic processes, quotes Friedrich Schiller's statement, "If thou wouldst understand others, look into thine own heart!" We have within ourselves the same impulses and the same potentialities for experience that any other human being has. Only when we detect something familiar in our own experience, do we appreciate the quality of the other's experience which we have internalized. "I personally feel I only 'understand' if I can detect in my own mind the germ of a similar feeling as the one which I try to understand, given that a similar thing should happen to me" (Lumeij, 1957, p. 22).

It is important to note the important qualification that Lumeij introduces. It is not essential that we experience the actual event. We can imagine the event and anticipate what our own response might be. We have within ourselves the potentialities of every human response. Because we share this common emotional endowment, we are able to understand from within ourselves what the meaning of the experience of others might be for them. We could not recognize the other's experience unless we had some *a priori* knowledge of it.

Reik wrote of our own responses as "signposts" which point to "the unconscious motives and secret purposes of the other person." Our own responses may not be identical with others. There will be points of smilarity because of the sameness of endowment. At the same time there will be points of different emphasis too, because of differences in constitution and experience. Similarities and differences become equally important signposts of understanding.

The psychoanalyst's emotional integrity becomes a touchstone for the mental and emotional integrity of his patient. There is no other way for him to evaluate the unconscious processes of others except by this process of comparison. It is obvious that the therapist must have a greater degree of psychological insight. If he shared the identical experience completely, he would certainly have the "feel" of the experience of his patient, but he could have little insight into the possible distortions of his patient's reactions. This stage in the empathic process is more unconscious than conscious. The empathizer does not consciously assess what is similar or dissimilar in his own responses and those of others. He does not initiate the alternation between his reason and his fantasy. The process of vibration is an involuntary activity which might be located in the preconscious. The awareness that accrues is implicit rather than explicit. The empathizer has become engaged in play activity which he does not seek to control. If he interrupts the process of vibration prematurely, he is likely to impede the interaction of his own feelings and his reason. If he becomes deliberate and serious too soon, the communication on deeper levels is blocked, and his understanding remains less personal and more intellectual. He remains involved, attached, and identified long enough to allow for his personal reactions to be evoked and for deeper levels of his own unconscious to be stimulated.

(4) DETACHMENT. In this phase of empathic understanding, we withdraw from our subjective involvement and use the methods of reason and scrutiny. We break our identification and deliberately move away to gain the social and psychic distance necessary for objective analysis. We try to place our understanding in a perspective. To do this, we must in a sense eject the ego that we had previously introjected.

In the disciplined attempt to compare and to analyze, some facets and qualities of our understanding are inevitably lost. They remain within the comprehension of the empathizer, who cannot adequately put them into verbal symbols or categories to facilitate sharing discoveries and conclusions with others. Drawing on his intellectual capacities, the empathizer makes comparisons between the data he has gained and information derived from other sources. In this phase the anthropologist would exchange notes with his colleague, trying to fit his new knowledge into a kind of intelligible pattern consistent with other published studies. The therapist would compare his own data with the data of the clinical psychologist or with facts about the patient that had been obtained from members of the patient's family or from the family physician. There could be no substitute, in this phase, for intellectual clarity and for full awareness of all available data. The power of dispassionate analysis is as essential in this phase as was the power to identify deeply in phases (1) and (2).

Illustrating the Model

Any illustration of the full cycle of empathic understanding requires an explicit description of the complex series of intra-psychic responses. However, the movement of introspective and imaginative processes is so rapid that no static verbal statement could possibly capture it. The following outline does not make possible a re-experiencing of what the therapist himself experiences. It is not intended to evoke the empathic responses of the reader as much as it is to give him an intellectual and conceptual grasp of a more complete sequence of empathic understanding by a therapist.

This example illustrates a fragment of understanding rather than a comprehensive or penetrating grasp of the emotional problems of the patient. A record of a series of highly empathic interviews over a continuous period would be necessary to illustrate such therapeutic insight. The following should be considered as a selection of material which is part of an extensive relationship between therapist and patient.

The therapist has previous knowledge of this patient. He has observed him on several previous occasions so that many of his gestures and nonverbal cues already form part of the therapist's knowledge of the patient. His empathic activity is therefore stimulated by past associations as well as by spontaneous responses to the words and feelings now being expressed in the face-to-face meeting. In column one we describe briefly the different kinds of participation by the client. Column two reports

some of the overt responses of the therapist as well as some examples of his imaginative activity. In column three, we classify
the therapist's responses, both interpersonal and intrapsychic, in
terms of the four phases: (1) *Identification* (assuming the identity
of the other); (2) *Incorporation* (introjecting the ego of the
other); (3) *Reverberation* (vibrating in the rhythm of the other
and one's own rhythm at the same time); and (4) *Detachment*
(ejecting the ego of the other and withdrawing to analyze and
compare). Some responses represent combinations of specific
phases. In the intermediate stages of empathic understanding the
interaction of the subject and the object is rapid and we should
not expect to find a sequential movement from one distinct
phase to another. The categories can be tidily separated in a
conceptual scheme but not in the empathic experience itself. In
general, however, there is a movement from objectivity to identification and back again to the original social distance or detachment.

The situation concerns a student nearing the end of his preparation for a professional career. His physical symptoms are
weakness, tremulousness, and extreme fatigue. He has sought
psychological help because he feels inhibited from making a
successful work adjustment and is anxious about the responsibilities of his approaching professional assignment.

This sketchy illustration of the sequence of empathic understanding is made after the fact, so to speak. The therapist draws
on his memory and tries to report as much as he can reproduce
of the stream of conscious and preconscious activity within him
as he faced his client. Even if we allow for a degree of rationaliza-
tion and of some errors in reconstructing the original empathic
experience, we are able to observe the way in which the therapist
merged and detached himself from the client. We also see the
alternation between the therapist's identification with the client
and his identification with himself as a child. The oscillation
among several identifications is quick and unpredictable.

The therapist re-experienced some of his own anxiety as a
child as he reverberated to the anxiety of his client. This subjective experience sharpened his awareness of what the client felt
and at the same time gave him a touchstone for evaluating the

Client	Therapist	Phase of Empathic Understanding
Voice is strained; eyes tearful, body agitated. Reports he cannot do his work—instructors make demands impossible for him to meet. Faces calamity. Fears others will discover how weak he is.	Shortly after the opening comments by client, begins to feel slight depression and mild anxiety.	(1) and (2)
Talks of nervous breakdown. Pleads for help. Cannot muster any energy for work.	Experiences client's dread with a sense of reality.	(1)
Fears to attend his classes. Driven to take up every research suggestion made by instructor no matter how casually made.	Still immersed in the client's mood, senses some of his own feelings about authority figures, the mood of submission as well as actively seeking the approval of a superior.	(1), (2) and (3)
Makes an abrupt transition from the theme of the present conflict, associates to his childhood, and without explanatory comment relates memory of being beaten by his mother with a leather strap.	Vicariously feels the shame and rage of a child cowering under blows but enjoying in a desperate way the sense of power he has in being able to elicit such strong feelings from his mother; senses the ambivalence he himself had felt as a child.	(3)
Describes slipping to the ground. Mother stops beating him as he collapses. Says, "If I lay down, they will stop hitting me."	Aware that the client has rapidly alternated between his emotions when responding to his mother and his reference to the present in which he implies that if he regresses, the authorities will relax their demands upon him, replicating the situation of his childhood.	(3) and (4)

Client	Therapist	Phase of Empathic Under- standing
Begins to sob, repeats fear of a breakdown. Presents himself as hopeless but still reaches out for help.	Senses a theme of despair which is mixed with a certain lack of conviction about client's claim of utter helpless- ness.	(3) and (4)
	Assesses his re-experiencing of the patient's mood. Weighs this insight in light of objec- tive knowledge he has of the client. Associates to these data in terms of psychoanalytic concepts of Oedipal anxiety. Asks what defenses are being used.	(4)
	Asks student if he thinks be- coming ill will induce the instructors to reduce the pres- sure of his work. At same time senses that the student has already become aware of his own repetition compulsion and is at the point of being able to understand his own mech- anisms of defense.	(4) and (1)
	Asks student if he is fearful that he will now use a tactic about which he is somewhat ambivalent. Also asks if stu- dent is still attached to his original goals in taking up his professional preparation.	(1) and (4)

response of the client. The therapist had the same impulses to attack and to yield, but he becomes aware of the fact that he did not act on these impulses in the same way. In his own ex- perience he did not develop and refine this method of dealing with his own ambivalent emotions. He recognized how dissatisfied the client must be with the impulse to use the familiar defense mechanism which is currently so inappropriate. He could not appreciate the fear of the client that he would be unable to control those forces which seemed to push him toward regression. If he had been inclined earlier to take the client's complaints more literally and assume that the anxiety stemmed from a fear, partly real and partly distorted, of the punitive action of the authority figures, he now realized that the anxiety reflected fear of an impulse to regress.

Even though the concluding phase of the interview was classified as "detachment," empathic elements were obviously present. The form of the comment to the client was logical. The therapist did not appear to be emotionally involved. He seemed to exemplify the professional self. But at that moment too, he was engaged in a process of identification. As he spoke, he put himself in the position of the client and in this way attempted to determine whether his choice of words was suitable and whether or not the affect in his voice and manner was sensitive and reassuring. It is obvious that in the concluding phase we ought to speak of greater detachment rather than convey the idea that the empathizer has withdrawn completely from the field of the other person. The other person remains a person and not an object. In the therapeutic use of empathic understanding, we are aware of shifts between greater or lesser objectivity, but we always assume a human and personal engagement.

Problem Solving (Dewey) and Empathic Understanding (Reik)

There are some points of comparison between this model of empathic understanding and the five steps which John Dewey specified in explaining how we think. The rigorous and disciplined logician Dewey also allowed for the play of the imagination. His reference to a "rhythm of the unconscious and the conscious" as the source of fruitful thinking seems close to the more psychoanalytic explanation given by Reik of the creative process in empathic understanding. Dewey describes the ideal mental condition as being "playful and serious at the same time" (1910, p. 218). Reik's formula of empathic understanding as an equilibrium of involvement and detachment is paralleled by Dewey's discussion of an alternation between projection and reflection, "a process of going directly ahead and of turning back in scrutiny." The philosopher recommended that in at least one phase of the process of logical reflection we must suspend our intellectual alertness and allow for the play of fantasy and suggestion. The model of empathic understanding can be seen as an elaboration of the intermediate processes between projection and reflection.

Dewey's formula of thinking did not specify the element of *Einfühlung* or identification of the thinker with the object. Although he did not use the term "subjective understanding," he seems to have implied something of the kind when he stressed the distinctions between unconscious and conscious processes. Both the subjective and the objective, the unconscious and the conscious, are necessary. One activity gives spontaneity and the other, control. The positions of Dewey and of Reik are in agreement on this point.

An outline of the formulas given by the philosopher and the psychoanalyst indicates some points of similarity:

Dewey on Thinking	Reik on Listening with the Third Ear	
I Feeling a difficulty.	(1)	Identification.
II Locating and defining it.	(2)	Incorporation.
III Suggesting possible solutions.		
IV Developing the bearings of the solutions by reasoning.	(3)	Reverberation.
V Further observing and experimenting to determine acceptance or rejection of the suggested solution.	(4)	Detachment.

The final steps in both cases involve familiar scientific and logical thought. The phase of reverberation (3) of Reik seems to parallel phases III and IV of Dewey, particularly if we keep in mind that Dewey defended the logic of the unconscious. His reference to the suggestion of possible solutions did not imply the self-conscious thought processes of step V. He had in mind a playful indulgence in fantasy activity, which we can consider analogous to the inner activities of the empathizer as he experiences the interaction between the alter ego he has identified with and his own native personality. Reik points out that we cannot predict what will emerge from deeper levels of personality as a result of such reverberations. Dewey too pointed out that in the activity of the imagination in step III, there is a "leap, jump, the propriety of which cannot be absolutely warranted in advance." It goes without saying that the objective of reflective thinking—which is problem-solving of a general kind—and the objective of empathic understanding—which is the solving of psychological problems and the grasping of inner psychic reality—are not completely comparable. Understanding people is a specialized task in the general problem of comprehension and calls for more than the usual investment of self in the subject or the object being studied.

It was essential to distinguish between the sophisticated process of empathic understanding and simple empathy. We now need to inquire into the specific nature of the empathic skill, the subjective and emotional capacity that is so obscure and so problematic.

Theodor Reik pointed to one of the major issues in comprehending empathy when he wrote:

It is hard to form any idea of the psychological nature of empathy, for in the controversy over the conception the process appears sometimes as the natural, unconscious condition of psychological comprehension, sometimes as the result of a special effort and conscious endeavor (1949, p. 357).

If empathy is "natural and unconscious," it may derive from innate capacities in man and represent a more primitive and instinctive form of understanding. On the other hand, it may be an archaic and nonrational capacity which is also accessible to

training. Whether empathy is a product of biological endowment or is derived from socialization and learning processes or
a combination of both factors is, of course, a problem that bears
on the empathy variable among individuals. How do we account
for the fact that there is such a diversity of empathic powers?
Allowing even that the social situation itself is an important
variable in successful empathy, we are still confronted with the
fact that individuals vary in their capacity for empathy. Research
in social psychology has already indicated that empathy is correlated negatively with ethnocentrics, with projectors, with hypo-
chondriacs, and with psychopaths. It is positively correlated with
personalities who are equalitarian, who are insightful, and who
are spontaneous. Empirical research in the measurement of different capacities for empathy has been published. The fact that
such differences exist is indisputable. The theoretical question—
at least as important—is the source of the variable. Do some individuals have a constitutional defect in empathizing? Do others
have certain life experiences which enhance whatever native
capacity they have? We require an understanding of the full
range of forces that can possibly determine the empathic capacity
of a given individual. We also require a greater appreciation of
the blind spots which prevent the practitioner from using his own
empathic powers with more versatility. We are curious, too,
about those interpersonal attitudes and those skills in social and
psychological observation which affect the success of our empathic activities.

Even if no one can be taught to empathize any more than he
can be taught to hear a tonal pattern (to use an illustration applied originally by Gordon Allport in reference to gaining intuitive skills), one can be taught to listen to and look for
significant features in an empathic relationship that is spontaneously established. This study addresses itself to that possibility.

III

THE EMPATHIC SKILL

FEW IF ANY comprehensive theories of the origin and operation of empathy have been offered in any one of the many disciplines—from biology to aesthetics—that treat this phenomenon. Committed to no particular school of thought, we are free to range over the field, selecting relevant ideas and following promising leads. This approach yields clues to the mystery of the empathic skill. The meaning of some facets of empathy may still elude our grasp, but we aim to allow as few leads as possible to go unnoticed.

Two large as well as several minor questions confront us. They will serve as guidelines through the different disciplines and sources that we intend to mine for clues and insights. First, to what extent is the empathic skill a more primitive, biological capacity and to what extent is it a combination of innate and learned behavior? Second, through what channels of mind and body does the empathic skill function? One question deals with origins; the other, with modes of operation. Another question, no less important but even more difficult to answer, concerns the issue of projection versus reality. Do we actually feel into the other person? In what sense can imitation be said to be a form of participation in the experience of a separate personality? Partial or more complete answers to such questions as these will not only advance our scientific knowledge but also provide intelligent direction in the training of therapists and researchers. We learn what can and what cannot be changed when we try to control the factors that inhibit or promote the successful exercise of this mode of communication.

In beginning a detailed examination of the empathic skill, we must keep in mind the principle that empathy is based on a feeling of similarity. The question that intrudes itself is from where do we initially derive such a sense of familiarity or recognition. When we empathize we do no more than extend or deepen a basic minimum of understanding that we already have of the experience of the other person. The potential is already there. We must have some common ground of understanding or basis for mutual appreciation. Empathy is a skill which helps us fulfill a potential. It brings to life, so to speak, a sense of appreciation which had been there before. This feeling of familiarity may derive from a common biological endowment. It may also derive from the fact that both the subject and the object have had the same or comparable life experiences. In either case, the logic is the same. To be able to recognize something, we require some form of *a priori* knowledge.

Unless we had some familiarity with the experiences of others, we would be unable to recognize or identify their experiences. If we projected ourselves into the mind of another person and literally took his viewpoint, how would we know that what we saw with his eyes is a book or a telephone? If we felt ourselves into his emotions, how would we know that this heavy and uncomfortable sensation is "grief"? The anthropologist Redfield makes the same point regarding scientific research. In order to know what a Zuñi Indian is ashamed of, one must first know what it means to be ashamed. Redfield's simple but basic point is worth noting:

The simple fact seems to be that to study and to report the way of life of another people one must begin by assuming, as common sense assumes in trying to reach understanding in talking with another person, that something is the same in that way of life and one's own. One cannot listen meaningfully to another without supposing that there is something in his way of conceiving things and of judging that is the same as one's own (1955, p. 93).

What are the sources of this similarity? If they are a matter of common biological endowment, then empathy is possible without our having had the same experiences. It is almost independent of experience. This similarity may also depend upon identical or comparable experiences. To account for empathy, which is a process of achieving a sense of even greater similarity, we presuppose some kind of *a priori* sameness.

In this chapter we have a double objective. We look for the sources of such *a priori* knowledge, tracing the channels through which this similarity is sensed. We explore the ways that both constitution and environment interact, speculating how physical and nonphysical or imaginative senses can be involved.

Variations in Empathic Skills

Individuals with empathic insights into members of their group often differ among themselves in degrees of empathic power. The level of empathy is not the same for every Negro just because he is a Negro or for each member of a peer group simply because he belongs to the group. Shall we account for such differences by observing that a social experience for one person is never the same as it is for another? Situations and circumstances are not completely repetitive; thus, individuals cannot respond to stimuli that are constant. Could we think of two individuals experiencing the same event under the same conditions, we would still find that one of the dyad would have more empathic insight than the other. Beyond a certain level of mutual appreciation there would be subtle but important variations in the skill of empathizing. Something more than situational factors must account for differences in empathy.

The empathic variable extends over a spectrum which ranges from the deep empathies of a Shakespeare to the fixed and self-centered perspective of a schizophrenic personality. Shakespeare had the capacity to identify with a vast number of individuals. He possessed a fertile imagination and the ability to leap from one identification to another. He could faithfully portray a gamut of characters because he must have been flexible enough to abandon temporarily his own identity. Shakespeare must have been a man with deep and far-ranging personal experiences as well as being spectacularly endowed with intuitive power.

The psychotic personality, on the other hand, has little or no ability to take the role of others. No matter how hard he may try, the psychotic is unable to take the perspective of the other person. He cannot understand the inner states of others and is like a stranger who does not speak the same language. He is unable to sense a similarity between himself and others. Because he is estranged from himself and his own emotions, he is unable to feel intimacy with others; he is disassociated both from himself and from others. It is said that exceptional schizophrenics reveal an uncanny ability to understand other persons. They appear to apprehend the feelings of others, to penetrate the subtle conflicts or problems in the personalities of their therapists. But such cases are exceptions to the rule. When they do occur, they are examples of the principle that psychological recognition depends upon similarity of knower and subject; we identify in others the experiences or psychological states already familiar to us. Schizophrenics occasionally become aware of points of similarity between their own conflicts and conflicts in others, but this capacity is often distorted. They do not share the same meanings and shift their frame of reference. They are not sure enough of their own identity to risk the "letting go" that is necessary in empathizing.

Still another variation is seen in the phenomenon of excessive empathy. In certain mental states the individual feels that his ego extends beyond himself and engulfs other people and other objects almost completely. He is aware of no distinction between himself and others. Psychotic empathy of this kind is observable in severely ill patients, but is also observable among otherwise normal individuals who experience an exaggerated empathy under the effect of drugs like mescaline. In delusory empathy induced by drugs, the individual loses the *as-if* capacity and feels that he has merged with his environment. There is a loss of ability to distinguish between symbol and reality. In acts of what we might call more normal empathy, we become fused with the identities of others, although this is but a transient experience. We catch ourselves on the side of the other for just a moment. Under the influence of drugs, we experience a sense of similarity or relatedness that is like a mystic or orgiastic union. The drug releases inhibitions to imitative impulses. It also induces an intense regression to earlier states of existence when we were part of larger wholes and had no existence separate from other individuals or to earlier states in history when our existence was primarily collective or tribal. A sense of primal unity, either biological or historical, revives under such stimulation.

It is obvious that individuals vary in their empathic abilities and we cannot help wondering with the novelist,

Why some men with talent, good will and compassion never achieve full human contact and raise only contention and ridicule among those they try to help. And why others, with no apparent effort, walk straight into intimacy and are remembered with love long after their death (Morris L. West, 1959, p. 100).

But we are also curious about the course that the empathic ability takes within a specific person. Does it atrophy and decline, or develop and reach out widely? If empathy is an instinctual form of understanding, it may decline as the individual matures. We learn to put aside more primitive methods of communication. We come to rely on our secondary or acquired abilities to reason and to use symbols. Those who stress the secondary or learned character of empathy differ in their views of the course its development takes. Some point out that the individual soon learns to conform to established and stereotyped images. He develops sufficient empathy to become a member of the community and subsequently his empathic abilities are repetitive and superficial. Others suggest that the empathic ability can be enhanced. More of the individual's potential for empathy can be realized through training in role-taking and through deliberate efforts to break the mold of conformity.

Harry Stack Sullivan believed that empathy is a form of communication on a nonverbal level which can be traced back to the relationship of the infant to its mother. It is a direct and immediate apprehension of feelings in the other person. It is most intense in the infant, tending to decline with subsequent growth.

Empathy is the term we use to refer to the peculiar emotional linkage that subtends the relationship of the infant with other significant people. Long before there are any signs of understanding of emotional expression there is evidence of this emotional contagion or communion. We do not know much about the fate of empathy in the developmental history of people in general. There are indications that it endures throughout life, at least in some people (quoted in Blitsten, 1953, p. 79).

The social philosopher Max Scheler spoke of an instinct for specialized identification that is subject to atrophy in man. It was a residual capacity less common in the average civilized adult than "in primitive peoples, children, dreamers, neurotics of a certain type, hypnotic subjects and in the exercise of the maternal instinct" (Scheler, 1954, p. 31).

Freud suggested that identification (or empathy) was a method of communication or understanding that was subject to decline. His explanation is particularly interesting because it links understanding with the feeling of similarity. As the individual comes to feel less similar to objects and to other people, he finds identification to be less reliable.

without any special reflection we attribute to everyone else our own constitution and therefore our consciousness as well, and that this identification is a *sine qua non* of our understanding. This inference (or this identification) was formerly extended by the ego to other human beings, to animals, plants, inanimate objects and to the world at large, and proved serviceable so long as their similarity to the individual ego was overwhelmingly great; but it became more untrustworthy in proportion as the difference between the ego and these "others" widened (Freud, 1957b, p. 169).

The psychologist Ernest Schachtel draws both on biological and cultural factors to account for a decline in empathic abilities as the socialization of the child proceeds. He observed first a shift in the kind of senses used in communicating with the environment. The child first uses the "proximity senses" of taste, smell, and touch. He feels intimately involved in his environment. His senses give him direct participation. Even more, he feels that his own being is little distinguished from the beings of others. Gradually his culture, his parents, and teachers discourage his use of the proximity senses. Civilization gives preference to the eye and the ear for the purposes of communication. These are distance senses. The individual surrenders the use of those senses which brought him into intimate contact with others and now sees and hears people from a distance. More detached or alienated now, he feels that he is a subject and that others are objects, different from him. As a civilized adult, he becomes more estranged from his environment than he was as a more animal-like child. Schachtel (1959) suggests that culture also inhibits empathy by enforcing the use of conventional categories and images. The adults persuade the child to accept the standardized symbols of the culture. To the degree that he conforms, he surrenders his ability to relate spontaneously and directly. It is not inevitable, however, that our empathic abilities atrophy. In some individuals like poets, says Schachtel, the power to identify, to respond more sensitively, and to use a wider variety of images may never diminish and may even increase.

The psychiatrist Moreno suggests that exercises in psychodramatic techniques can evoke latent empathic powers. Through training in role-playing the individual learns how to empathize more freely and also to correct distortions and blocks in the use of whatever empathic endowment he has.

The following survey of the determinants of empathy leads to a fuller appreciation of the biological and cultural factors which combine to give us a sense of similarity with others. In part, this similarity is innate. In part it is a case of social experience, a sharing of common human conditions, which intensifies and extends an *a priori* likeness. Between differences in biological endowment and differences in life history, we are likely to account for the phenomenon of an empathy variable.

Biological Factors

We can give weight to the role of biological and more social or psychosocial factors without setting up an either-or distinction between the two. Some authorities do emphasize one determinant. For the social psychologist empathic ability develops with social experience, while for the biologist it is an archaic mode of communication almost entirely instinctive. In Freud we find a balancing of the constitutional and the environmental. Since social scientists tend to make history and environment predominant, it is all the more essential to consider what determinants of the empathic ability, if any, are independent of experience.

AUTONOMOUS CAPACITY. A simple way to explain the origin of the empathic skill is to postulate that we are born to understand. Part of our biological heritage is the capacity to visualize and to apprehend the feelings of other members of our species. We do not locate this ability in a particular sense organ. It is simply a function of our inner senses, an imaginative or intuitive gift which is part of human nature.

This conception has proved satisfactory for such thinkers as Ferenczi, Adler, Scheler, Buber, and Murphy. All of them take for granted an innate potentiality for comprehending the feelings of others. For Ferenczi, a psychologist, the empathic ability is located in the unconscious where each man has a "virtual potentiality for sympathetic sensitivity" (Ferenczi, 1955, p. 154). Like the social philosophers, Scheler and Buber, Adler located the empathic capacity in a basic relatedness that is part of the cosmos itself. Whereas Ferenczi would speak of the unconscious as a catch-all term, Adler would refer to the innate "social feeling" (Adler, 1927, p. 61). These psychiatrists explained empathy in terms of their basic conceptions of personality structure.

In the case of the more philosophical Scheler, we find the substitution of the term "genuine fellow-feeling" for empathy. Since we are obliged to agree that empathy is possibly physical or motor (the position of Scheler and Buber), we can include Scheler's idea of the innate and autonomous character of "fellow-feeling" in our present discussion of the biological origins of empathy. For him, the ability of one man to participate in the emotional experience of another is an innate capacity independent of experience. He made a distinction between comprehending the basic emotions of another person and appreciating certain sensory or physical experiences. He observes that the Occidental does not automatically share the enthusiasm of the Japanese for raw fish. Such tastes are not innate. Such tastes would have to be educated. The appreciation is not direct and immediate. With respect to more subtle emotional states, however, no common culture or shared experiences are prerequisite for empathizing; the capacity is autonomous. The basis of our similarity is a common humanity. Through the exercise of our imaginative and sympathetic powers, we are able to make this innate similarity become more vivid and real. The "in-group" we belong to is humanity itself, not a particular tribe or community with a particular history.

Given the range of emotional qualities of which man is intrinsically capable, and from which alone his actual feelings are built up, he has an equally innate capacity for comprehending the feelings of others, even though he may never on any occasion have encountered such feelings (or their ingredients) in himself, as really unitary experiences (Scheler, 1954, p. 48).

For the psychologist Murphy, empathy is a basic gift or capacity of men to love one another. He does not range into metaphysics as does Buber, who speaks of an "original awareness" of the Thou, a condition of *a priori* readiness for meeting with others. To Murphy, empathy is a case of a primitive resonance between two human beings. There is something fundamentally similar between others and ourselves. When we respond and accept one another, something basic to our own nature resonates to the same core in the other person.

An autonomous empathic capacity might suitably be called *primordial empathy*. It could not be empirically demonstrated. We might well conceptualize it by the term "archetypal." Jung's theory of archetypes, difficult in itself to appreciate or to defend, does give us some feeling for a phenomenon that is part of the biological heritage of the species. Individuals share the same archetypes of basic emotional states and therefore enjoy the potentiality for the same emotions.

It is not essential that each have comparable experiences so long as they have a built-in apparatus which gives them an almost direct comprehension of the other. For one thing we have the same inner strivings conditioned by a common endowment. Even though our life experiences may differ and our characters develop in different patterns, the instinctual readiness is present, so that the scholar can understand the peasant, and the generous spender the miser. We do not experience the same things, writes the sociologist Watson,

yet nothing that men do is utterly foreign to our inner selves. The basest crimes, or the noblest heroism, grow in the same soil as our own less notable actions. We too have lived with the same impulses. And the more surely we have learned to know and to heed these forces in ourselves, the sounder will be our grasp of mankind—even in its strangest extravagances (1953, pp. 53-54).

In discussing the operation of the empathic skill as a function of the imagination, as we shall do in more detail, we presume an ability to visualize the experiences and sensations of others. We can conceive of the actions as well as the motives of others because we have within ourselves at least the potentiality for the same experience. We are two of a kind in terms of physique as well as impulse. We appreciate the graceful movements of a Pavlova, Rebecca West wrote, not because we can dance as well but because we have the same muscular structure (1928, p. 101). We can appreciate the motives of the saint and the criminal because to some degree we share the same endowment, even though our potentialities took different courses of development.

ONCE WE WERE ONE. We become more sympathetic to the principle of primordial empathy if we think of humanity as evolving out of a common source. Before we existed as individuals, we were part of a larger whole. Even though we have achieved a measure of separateness or individuality, we still carry traces of our original genetic unity. If we are able to recognize the emotions of others, we are actually engaging in an act of *re-cognition*. We are recalling something that we once knew. An earlier sense of unity is reawakened so that we identify in others something that originally united others and ourselves.

There are many ways of thinking about the original unity of mankind. For the philosopher it is an original moral unity; for the geneticist, a common life-substance; for the social psychologist, a flow of experience before the dam of selfhood has been built; for the psychoanalyst, a common element that remains in the unconscious. The basic resemblance which is central to empathy derives from a common, undifferentiated ego. "The ego-feeling we are aware of now is thus only a shrunken vestige of a far more extensive feeling—a feeling which embraced the universe and expressed an inseparable connection of the ego with the external world" (Freud, 1961, p. 68). At those moments when we apprehend the feelings of others empathically, our own ego, to use Freudian terms, has expanded so that it experiences once more the sense of being part of a larger unit of being. We lose awareness of our individuality as we recover our sense of original participation in a common existence.

The principle that "once we were one" helps us to understand the regressive element in empathy. We slip back to earlier stages in our development when the child lived in the mother and had no sense of separate existence. The individual relives earlier stages of his development. He sloughs off his recently acquired ego and once again feels connected to another being. He no longer experiences himself as an object and becomes merged with a more comprehensive and unitary existence.

We can understand the process of empathy itself much more clearly if we recognize that in the temporary loss of self-awareness the empathizer follows the channels of a more primitive experience. Murphy's analysis is very much to the point:

The motor, and consequently the kinaesthetic, tendencies follow the stimulus patterns without regard to their assigned status as *your* or *my* behavior; empathy and mimicry follow channels of earlier experience without any need to ask whose effort or activity is in progress (1947, p. 382).

There is no question of conscious analogy between your experience and mine. An original sense of identity, or oneness of feeling and being, is reinstated and re-experienced. The dichotomy of self and society which gradually developed as the child moved away from the mother now disappears. We are once more "possessed" by an original more encompassing being. The more primary and elemental experience of participation in a common body is possible once again. At the same time as the motor tendencies are stimulated, the more subtle, less tangible activities of the inner senses or the imagination are evoked. The sense of participation is as real as the physical imitation or the motor empathy. We resonate psychologically as well as kinaesthetically.

It would be possible, if we chose to follow Freud's speculations about a tribal or a racial unconscious, to think of an original unity of experience. We have within our own unconscious a memory of primitive stages of man's history. Traces of these memories may persist as residual deposits which in moments of empathy come more forcibly to dominate our awareness. In some recess of the unconscious which is common to all men the earliest experiences of the race are preserved. Atavistic fears and anxieties as well as longings for reaffiliation may be re-experienced. The sense of a tribal *mystique*, a feeling of living collectively rather than individually, survives in more obvious forms in primitive tribes even today.

Civilization which stresses a sense of detachment is nowhere able to root out completely the traces of this more primitive, participating mentality, in which individuals are not aware of ego boundaries. The concept of a group ego, biologically transmitted, helps account for the origin of empathy. When we feel into the other person, we become more conscious of an archaic and original unity and we recognize the ego that is common to both. Nothing in a fellow human being can really be alien to us. When we are stimulated by the experiences of others, we recollect the original experience of living as parts of a whole. Psychological understanding can therefore be considered a form of self-recollection. Such recollection may involve a regression beyond the uterine experience of the child back into the primitive stages in the evolution of the race. All psychological knowledge is therefore unitary. Men become forgetful and in regressive empathy they retrieve some of the lost knowledge of their own nature which is at the same time the nature of every other human being.

Two OF A KIND. In their study of communication, Ruesch and Bateson observed that "empathic assessment" becomes possible between two individuals because they share the same anatomical, physical, and sensory structure.

Each person must at least have some notions about himself and the other; he must, for example, think of both as alike in being alive and capable of emitting and receiving communication. Indeed, if misunderstanding leads to hostility, it is immediately clear that there must exist common premises regarding anger and pain. The beginnings of a common codification system are latent in our biological nature, our common anatomy and common experience of bodily function and maturation (1951, pp. 203-204).

Men communicate with each other because they share the same impulses and have a common codification system. It is not essential that both have the same experiences so long as they have a built-in apparatus which gives them a more direct comprehension of each other. There is evidence of a more empirical kind of methods of communication we may call empathic in the codification system of animals. It is more primitive and more instinctual than the more complex symbolic systems of men which require years of social experience. The principle of such communication is the same whether we respond as cats to an arched spine or whether we respond as humans to a smile or to the succession of verbal symbols in the memorable phrases of a Churchill. When we have the same response or attach the same meaning to the same cue, gesture, or verbal symbol, we are able to share messages and communicate effectively. From the evidence of Darwin, Köhler, and more contemporary research in animal communication as that being done by Lorenz, it is clear that animals have a large repertory of built-in cues that make instant recognition and communication possible. In the human animal, many of these innate sensitivities have atrophied and those that still survive, like the empathy of the infant for the anxiety of the

mother which Sullivan described, tend to diminish with maturation
and socialization. Certain forms of direct intuition and nonverbal
communication in the human animal are vestiges of communication systems which are more fully preserved in other animal
forms.

There are many indications of instinctive responses to the
same cues which lead biologists to believe that animals understand
each other's gestures and expressions. Charles Darwin collected an
impressive series of illustrations of the behavior of both animals
and men. The erection of hair and the dilation of pupils signal
fear. Uncovering of the canine tooth telegraphs hostility, as does
spitting and the ejection of the tongue. The furrows on the fore-
head are universally recognized as the grief muscles, while the
laugh and the smile are part of a common endowment. When we
avert or close our eyes we communicate to the other person the
thought that we consider him hardly worth looking at. To turn
up the nose is to indicate that we respond to the other person
as an unpleasantly smelling object. Darwin observed that one of
the basic meanings of scorn is ordure, recalling the common impulse to consider an unpopular person as dirt. We communicate
pride by raising ourselves to an erect position in the manner of a
peacock. The indication of approval or disapproval is conveyed
by the appropriate shaking of the head. Darwin was impressed
by the reliability as well as the universality of such symbolic
systems. "They reveal the thoughts and intentions of others more
truly than do words, which may be falsified" (1955, p. 364).

More recent animal research has extended the pioneering observations of Darwin and brought to light subtle processes of
instinctive communication. One example is the process of disarm-
ing by vulnerability. In a struggle, the losing animal will save
itself from being destroyed by the aggressor animal by an act
of complete submission that will be immediately recognized
and accepted. A vulnerable area of the loser's body, a top of the
head or the fleshy part of the neck is presented to the attacker. The
central nervous system of the aggressor responds directly to this
presentation and inhibits the expression of the instinct to kill.
Both partners in the engagement instinctively appreciate the
meaning of the gesture (Lorenz, 1952, pp. 195-196). Flashes of
sudden insight into the behavior of others which cannot be ac-

counted for on the basis of overt cues may be instances of the survival in man of such instinctive mechanisms. The awareness of the infant of the mother's anxiety might be an example of such primitive, animal-like comprehension. Some adults may still retain such forms of archaic, preverbal recognition.

NATURAL IMITATORS. An essential part of the biological system of communication is readiness to imitate. One animal imitates the gesture or the emotional expression of another and by this act of imitation evokes the emotional response of the other animal in itself. In lower forms of life, as birds and fish, the mimetic impulses are stronger than in the mammals. But even in man the tendency to imitate survives in the form of an innate readiness to respond to others, to associate to their gestures and moods, and to be suggestible to their influence. The infant has a built-in sensitivity to the actions and cues of others. Much of his mimicking derives from his social experience, but the basic sensitivity and openness to suggestion are built in.

Closely associated with the impulse to mimic is the instinct for play. We have an organic need for actively using our sensory equipment and our imagination. Both lower and higher forms of life engage in forms of playful imitation when they take the parts of others and demonstrate an innate capacity for *as-if* behavior. By its very nature, play calls for a relaxation of the normal alertness and readiness for fight or flight. The animal in play exhibits a greater flexibility of response and at the same time is capable of responding with greater sensitivity to a wide range of stimuli. In play we are more suggestible. We throw ourselves into the activity with self-abandon and become wrapped up in the game or in the identity of the person or object that we imitate. Imitation is therefore linked to identification.

A path leads from identification by way of imitation to empathy, that is to the comprehension of the mechanism by means of which we are enabled to take up any attitude at all toward another mental life (Freud, 1955b, p. 110).

Tendencies to imitate, to play, and to dramatize may express themselves in overt activity of the body. Our faces assume the expression of our neighbor. We feel the blow that the boxer has landed in the stomach of his opponent. There is a form of inner imitation also in our imagination. When we inwardly imitate, we are participating vicariously, even though it is hard to locate the activity in a particular sense organ. Our imaginative identification with the dramatic actor is a playful, partly spontaneous activity of the same order as our kinaesthetic imitation of the athlete.

The empathic skill is often described as archaic, primitive, or instinctive because it precedes the more cultivated use of secondary processes of thought. It is a "natural" or automatic form of communication because it involves more of the instinctive apparatus which still forms part of the human equipment. The impulse to imitate and to engage in playful activity—both physical and imaginative—are both parts of the biological endowment. They play a larger part in empathy than they do in the more secondary processes of thinking and analysis.

It is difficult to determine whether sympathetic impulses should also be considered innate. Sympathy, like imitation, grows out of an instinctive readiness to respond to some stimulus in the behavior of another person. Lois Murphy suggested that children learn how and when to sympathize and with whom to sympathize, but the capacity for such parallel responses seems to be innate. "At least, distress when others are distressed seems primitive, naive, and reasonably universal, without inculcation by adults" (1937, pp. 295-296). The world is coextensive with ourselves and what affects the other evokes fellow-feeling in us. There is a strong element of association because the sight of another person's pain reawakens our memory of a similar pain. In terms of instinctive responses, empathy is close to sympathy. A distinction might be made between empathy as an immediate imitation and recognition of the other's behavior and sympathy as a reinstatement or reawakening of a past experience of our own. When we empathize, we are less preoccupied with memories and associations and more free to lose ourselves in imitating others. To this extent empathy is more purely and directly spontaneous and sympathy, more a matter of conditioned reflex.

Another biological element of the empathic skill is the capacity for emotional affiliation. We tend not only to imitate or to vibrate in harmony with others but also to feel instinctively driven to affiliate with others, to relate with affection, and to support one another. It would be difficult to distinguish between the sympathetic, mimetic, and affiliative instincts. The existence of a basic fellow feeling can be inferred from the existence of a group ego or a common biological heritage. We are drawn to others by a need to re-establish an original unity that was lost. Such affiliative strivings can be a regression to the state of symbiotic union with the mother or a more primitive, innate instinct to reinstate earlier stages in the history of the race.

Freud and Identification

Freud's concept of identification combines the biological factors just outlined with the cultural experiences stressed by George Herbert Mead. For the psychoanalyst, identification is an unconscious activity based on the instincts and is conditioned by childhood experiences. Mead, as we shall see, interpreted identification and empathy as a form of role-taking, a technique enabling the child to learn and experiment. It is more of a rational or a secondary process. Freud, on the other hand, allowed for a larger play of instinctual activity.

From Freud we learn the functions of identification and gain insight into its constituent processes. The human animal has an instinctive need to identify because it is impelled to consume and to possess, to defend itself against stronger figures and to recover or repeat what was lost in earlier, more secure conditions of existence. We use identification to achieve a sense of self or ego. We also use it in different degrees as a defense against the anxiety of dependence, weakness, and loneliness.

The elements of identification include introjection, imitation, and regression. They form part of a unitary process by which we establish a feeling of similarity or equivalence with others. Whether identification is used appropriately depends upon the life experiences of the child. In the healthy personality, identification serves usually as a means of getting the other person's viewpoint and makes harmonious and cooperative relationships possible. Successful childhood experiences in identifying with others help the individual acquire a sense of his own identity. He comes to experience himself as a worthwhile person and learns to enjoy intimacy and association with others. He is free, as a normal adult, to establish warm identifications and to communicate with others, sensitive to his own needs as well as to theirs. When used more pathologically, however, identification is either meager as in the case of the sociopath who has no reliable sense of the feelings of others or is almost entirely deficient, as in the case of the psychotic who cannot abandon his own rigid frame of reference and fears that closeness to others will be damaging.

Although there are forms of hysterical identification in which the imitative activity is physical and overt, the psychoanalytic concept of the process usually designates an inner activity of the senses, the emotions, and the imagination. We again have evidence that empathic identification is by no means restricted to overt motor or kinaesthetic activity. It is primarily an inner (unconscious) activity and on this point Freud, the social psychologists, and the Lipps school of aesthetic empathy are largely in agreement.

One specific aspect of identification as interpreted by Freud is the cannibalistic instinct surviving in the impulse to introject the personality of the other person. The capacity for physical incorporation is part of the infant's basic endowment. He attempts to take in the objects of his environment by swallowing. Later he learns that he can enjoy and possess objects without physically incorporating them. He moves from physical assimilation to psychological introjection. He absorbs desired objects in a double process of introjection and imitation. The twin processes are closely associated. Freud's statement is notable: ". . . one ego becomes like another, one which results in the first ego behaving itself in certain respects in the same way as the second; it imitates it, and as it were takes it into itself" (1933, p. 90).

The child incorporates and imitates for two reasons. First, he wishes to take possession, and second, he wishes to resemble. The child feels inadequate and helpless and finds in the father figure a model of strength and authority. To overcome his own weakness, the child incorporates the strength of the father or imitates his features. He puts himself into his father's situation and unconsciously assumes his strength. The instinct for imitation is the first link in this process. The infant is able to mimic the adult by the time he has reached six months of age. Traces of this mimetic impulse are discernible even in the adult who uses baby talk in a regressive way in moments of somewhat self-conscious play with the infant.

The weakness of the child's position makes him more suggestible. He responds sensitively to the example of the stronger adult. He is driven along the path which leads from imitation to empathy, to use Freud's significant phrase, because it helps him avoid and conquer his own anxiety. A tendency toward identification, which is strong in the child, may also continue forcefully in older persons as a defense mechanism against anxiety in different situations. In the child, as in the adult, identification can express emotions of loving submission or of aggression. Identification is ambivalent and can express the need and character of a specific relationship.

A related phenomenon is the tendency of the weak or defenseless to identify with the aggressor. The child transforms himself into the punitive parental figure. The victim of the concentration camp identifies with the S. S. guard. Through this imitative process the individual makes himself similar to the feared object and vicariously escapes his own desperate destiny. The motive is defensive and hostile, but the same human capacity is involved here as in the more healthy and constructive identification which the growing child makes with the parent. In more normal identifications, the element of compassion and understanding outweighs the aggressive factor. Another variety of identification is the merging of the individual with the crowd. He loses his sense of individuality as he participates in the contagious excitement of the gang. Merged with the powerful group, he too feels his own anxiety diminished and achieves the sense of buoyancy and power that his new identity automatically gives him.

Regression is a related activity in the process of identification. We have the capacity for identifying not only with our contemporaries but also with persons who had once been significant to us and who persist in our memory. Regression is a form of retroactive identification. We recover old and familiar identities and re-experience identifications that were pleasant and reassuring. Through regression we relive the past, often impelled to do this because of current defeats or disturbing identifications. The activity is essentially repetitive. We revive older associations, earlier roles, and more familiar situations. The process is usually imaginative, but in more abnormal forms we act out our regressive identifications as well.

The impulse to regress can be viewed as part of an instinct for self-preservation. We want to hold on to what we once possessed. We keep the desired object near and alive by placing ourselves back in its earlier position. The varieties of regressive identification are many. We identify with loved figures whom we lost through death. We can revert to earlier roles and situations in our own biographies. The adult personality structure contains within it a whole series of identifications, both present and past. Through empathic powers the individual is able to move back and forth from one identity to another and from one ego state to another. We are able to "let go" of our tight hold on present reality and abandon our current role.

We reserve the term regression for the process of slipping back into identifications which have persisted in our unconscious. What is essential is not the direction of the shift but the fact that in empathic identification we have the basic capacity for moving from one identity to the other.

Whether regression is a healthy mechanism depends on the strength, duration, and purposes served. In situations of normal mourning we may make a temporary regressive identification with the lost person. "We become the lost person and we become again the person we were when the relationship was at its prime" (Erikson, 1954, p. 54). If we persist too long in such an identification, our regressive activity is an index of pathology. It is not unusual for normal adults to internalize persons for whom they mourn. They feel the deceased within them, re-experience his symptoms, and merge their own identity with his. By assimilating the characteristics of the dead, they unconsciously keep their hold upon him and keep him alive vicariously. Through such identification they are able to recover and retain the lost object.

So often used to describe a faulty technique of adaptation in the growing child, regression need not be associated only with ego weakness. It is part of the normal repertory of emotional expressions. In every act of empathy there is likely to be found some element of regressive behavior. We are moved to empathize because we want to reinstate something that once was part of ourselves. We sense something in the other person that is familiar, and by identifying with him we regain the sensation that was temporarily lost to us. Those who have no capacity for regression are inhibited in making identifications and in achieving empathic relationships. Their sense of personal identity may be so arbitrary on the one hand or so tenuous on the other that they may be unable to permit themselves even a minimum regressive attachment to others. The impetus to empathize may therefore be seen as an effort to recover something that was lost, a regressive recovery and re-experiencing of what was once familiar to us, if not actually a part of ourselves.

To introjection, imitation, and regression we might add a fourth component in the process of identification as interpreted by Freud. It is the unconscious recognition of our similarity with others. Freud once testified to the sense of empathy he had enjoyed with the Jewish group or community. He felt himself attracted to Jewry and to Jews because of a sense of identification he experienced with them. He believed that he participated in a community and shared with his fellow Jews not only a pride of common membership in a group but also a feeling of sameness or identity. The Jewish group, he believed, had something in common and a member of that group reflected in himself certain features of in-group empathy. He spoke of "obscure emotional forces" binding him to the group and "a clear consciousness of inner identity, the safe privacy of a common mental construction" —*Heimlichkeit der gleichen inneren Konstruktion* (1959c, p. 274). Freud's discussion of group psychology actually adds little to what we know as in-group empathy. Our recognition of others and the consequent identification we make with them grows out of our common membership in the same group, whether it be an army, a church, or a tribe. Freud listed a number of ways in which members of groups achieve a sense of similarity. Primitives partake of a totem and feel bound by this act to inhibit their aggressiveness and to practice mutual responsibility. They possess a common substance. Individuals who affiliate and choose to identify with a common leader or love-object come to experience a sense of mutual identification. "Originally rivals, they have succeeded in identifying themselves with one another by means of a similar love for the same object" (Freud, 1955b, p. 120). Freud accounts for the emotional contagion or hysterical identification among fellow members of a hospital ward as a recognition of something shared in common. A symptom will be imitated because one patient feels his problem is the same as that of the other patient whose behavior he observed.

Freud's major contribution to our understanding of empathy is his linking of the biological and the environmental or cultural factors. We move instinctively to empathize because we want to preserve ourselves by taking possession of objects and people we encounter in the present and also because we want to hold on to previous emotional satisfactions. We have the capacity to imitate, both physically and imaginatively. When we extend the range of our imitation over time and space into our past, we make regressive identifications. We allay our anxieties and fulfill our needs by reinstating earlier states of being. The stimulus of contact with some person or object that is intrinsically familiar evokes within us a chain of associations and makes it possible for us to reinstate the past. Freud's emphasis upon the role of childhood experience is particularly helpful in accounting for the empathy variable. Those who have made successful identifications retain the ability to empathize in adult life. In them the boundaries between one ego state and another or between conscious and unconscious processes are flexible or permeable. Traumatic early experiences lead to excessive or deficient empathizing. The boundaries can be too rigidly guarded or, on the other hand, too easily blurred. Even in the normal ego there lingers a readiness or a predisposition to regress to earlier and more pleasurable ego states.

George H. Mead and Role-Taking

We now turn from Freud and his ideas of identification to George H. Mead, a philosopher and social psychologist whose conceptions of role-taking add much to our understanding of the empathic skill. In fact, Mead's stress on the social and interpersonal aspects of communication affords a necessary balance to the psychoanalytic emphasis on the function of the instincts and the unconscious, nonverbal and emotional aspects of communication. The contrast between Freud and Mead helps us to understand the empathic skill as a combination of biological endowment and social experience. Both Freud and Mead dealt with the same phenomenon, although they stressed different aspects. The term "empathy" was specifically used by Freud in his association of empathy with identification and imitation. The term was not specifically used by Mead, although he described the empathic process. Writing of the process of taking the attitude of the other, Mead commented,

We feel with him and we are able so to *feel ourselves into the other* because we have, by our own attitude, aroused in ourselves the attitude of the person we are assisting (1934, p. 299. Italics ours).

A social psychologist, influenced by Mead, described the process as one

by which a person momentarily pretends to himself that he is another person, projects himself into the perceptual field of the other person, imaginatively puts himself in the other person's place, in order that he may get an insight into the other person's probable behavior in a given situation (Coutu, 1951, p. 180).

Another reference from the same author specifies "empathy":

Role-taking involves thinking and feeling as one believes the other person thinks and feels—a form of empathy or what might be called synconation (1951, p. 182).

The references here to thinking and feeling suggest that the conception of the empathic skill among social psychologists is closer to the technical cognitive process called "empathic understanding" which we discussed in the previous chapter. It is true that Mead considered role-taking to be more of a cognitive than an emotional phenomenon. At the same time he did not have in mind a sophisticated cognitive technique such as the psychoanalyst or the anthropologist would use. Role-taking (or empathy) interested Mead as a skill acquired in the process of general social interaction. It was a necessary function of the emerging personality, an instrument for developing a self and learning methods of adjusting to society. It was a basic facet of human communication, serving mainly as a method for planning actions, making decisions, and solving problems. In another sense, it was a technique by which we learn how to sympathize with other people and to assist by taking their attitudes. Even though Mead's concepts stress the cognitive and the intellectual aspects of communication, they properly belong in a discussion of the empathic skill. Empathy is largely a form of emotional communication, but not exclusively so. A review of the process of role-taking as a phase of self-development as well as symbolic communication in everyday relationships will add to our appreciation of the ways in which the practitioner draws on both his emotional and more intellectual capacities for communication. Mead himself insisted that role-taking was a form of communication by which we participate in the experience of another.

It is useful to compare psychoanalytic identification and role-taking with respect to such issues as motivation, biological determinants, methods of functioning, and the empathic variable. Freud took for granted the constructive role of identification in the process of ego development. The child forms an identity by imitating the parent. Freud was most concerned with empathic identification as a defensive tactic. The anxious individual overcomes his present weakness by identifying with powerful figures. He recovers the familiar and secure conditions of his past by making regressive identifications with objects and situations no longer present or with earlier and more primitive strata of his unconscious. Empathy is a security operation, to use Sullivan's discerning term.

The social psychologists see empathy as adaptive rather than reactive. Individuals imaginatively take the roles of others in order to anticipate behavior and to guide themselves in controlling their own actions. The process is a rehearsal for realistic and appropriate action. The other person is not so much a love-object as he is a fellow member of the team with whom one wishes to cooperate. It is not his person we wish to possess or to emulate but his ideas and his image of us that we wish to understand. He is a source for our own self-understanding, a mirror in which we are reflected. In taking his position we receive impressions of his image of ourselves so that we attain a more objective view. In this conception, role-taking serves a need for self-cognition and is far less an expression of affect-hunger.

Instinctual needs and emotional gratifications are far less prominent in Mead's theory. The individual develops techniques of self-adjustment through the process of imaginative role-taking. Experience teaches him how to anticipate the responses of the other and to control his own activity by the double process of injecting himself into the role of others and experimenting with the possible responses they might have to an action he is contemplating. Through role-taking the individual teaches himself to act more dispassionately and more self-consciously. "It is through taking this role of the other that he is able to come back on himself and so direct his own process of communication" (Mead, 1934, p. 254). Taking the role of the other does not carry with it the more profound emotional connotations of Freud's concept of identification or of Buber's principle of "inclusion." You imitate another's responses in a selective way. It is a more specialized activity, not only transient but confined to a specific situation and focused on the meaning of particular symbols. Mead did not rule out the emotional—he was simply more concerned with intellectual cognition than with the psychology of relationships or conflicts between instinct and culture.

Since he stressed the social nature of the human mind, it was natural for Mead to see role-taking as the method by which the growing child assimilated the images and symbols of society. Through this process the child developed a self or an ego that shared a common frame of reference and could therefore adapt itself to group life. The earliest evidence of role-taking in the history of the individual is the imitation of parents. When a child mimics the gestures and words of others, he is experimenting with new reactions. He learns how to compare and contrast the various meanings of certain activities to different people. The long period of dependence allows for many opportunities for such role experimentation, and not until late adolescence, as Erik

Erikson pointed out, is it necessary to make a decision about one's own role or sense of permanent identity.

In play activity, the child identifies temporarily with each figure that it imitates. Only gradually does the activity become more an organized game and less a random, individualistic act of play. The child learns the meaning of a number of roles and is gradually able to enact one role while being fully aware of the roles of other members and being capable of playing them all. In a game of baseball, Mead observed, the action of every player is based on an awareness of the potential responses of other members of the team. The child who learns how to play on the team has become an organized personality. His image of himself begins to take form because he has taken on others' roles and is able to see himself as others see him. His own personality becomes almost a composite of the images of himself which he has seen reflected in others. In Cooley's figure, the other person is the looking-glass in which we see ourselves; the outside view the mirror gives us is soon taken into ourselves and becomes the source of our own image of ourselves as persons. Without being able to inject ourselves into the roles of others and to gain reflexive awareness, we would have no sense of a separate and objective existence. Mead used the awkward term "the generalized other" to refer to the totality of social roles by which the individual judges his own actions.

Role-taking in Mead's terms was an internal, imaginative activity not to be confused with role-playing or psychodramatic methods in which roles are enacted on a stage, nor with the enactment of social roles in real life situations. Mead referred to inner processes of imagination and fantasy. In a conversation with others, role-taking would involve listening to what we ourselves say. This is not as paradoxical as it may sound. The statement we make to the other person is overt, audible, and actual. At the same time that we make this statement, we temporarily assume the role of our partner in the dialogue and listen to our words as they reach us in the new position that we will occupy for only a moment. We simultaneously speak and listen. We are the actor as well as the object to which the action is directed. This process of role-taking hinges upon the use of verbal symbols. Language connects others to ourselves. We hear our own words the way others hear them and are therefore able to understand what they mean to the other person. When our response and the response of the other person to the same word or symbol are similar or identical, we converse intelligently. We know the ideas and feelings of others because the word we direct to them has a similar meaning or effect upon us. If, for example, we quickly shout an alarm to a person who is in danger of stepping into the path of a fast-moving car, the words "look out" make us tense and prepare us too for the movement of jumping back. We do not perform the act, but our inner response is similar to the response of the person who hears our words and actually moves his body.

Thinking itself, as a form of solitary reflection, involves a similar kind of dialogue. Ideas suggest themselves and we try them out by carrying on an imaginary conversation with ourselves. We imagine how others would react. We oscillate from one alternative response to another through a process of reciprocal role-taking.

How might individual differences in role-taking ability be explained? Social psychologists would say that owing to faulty education or limited opportunities for role-experimentation, some individuals never internalize a sufficiently wide repertory of roles. They also fail to develop a sense of their own identity so that they have no basis for seeing themselves objectively. Lacking the ability to communicate with others, they cannot check and compare the different images others have of them. Those who adjust well receive a continuous flow of cues because they recognize the responses of others to them. They can imaginatively shift from the role of participant to observer and in this temporary suspension of overt activity they can experiment with different and more adaptive roles. Instead of alluding to deficiencies in innate empathic potential or the atrophy of archaic and primitive instincts for imitation, the more sociologically minded student of communication would interpret poor empathizing as a consequence of inadequate training in imaginative role-taking. Such an explanation does not conflict with a more psychoanalytic view. The Freudian school would press on to determine *why* a given individual did not use more effectively the kinds of opportunity he had for such learning and growth. Variations in instinctual endowment, affect hunger, and preverbal experience would also be given weight.

Jacob L. Moreno and Role-Playing

Still more light on the nature of the empathic skill is provided by the theory and practice of role-playing or psychodrama as developed by the psychiatrist, Jacob L. Moreno (1953). Here we find an emphasis on spontaneity and emotion which is close to Freudian thinking and a concern with roles and verbal symbols which is reminiscent of Mead's more rationalistic position.

From Moreno's empirical research and his program for therapeutic training we gain more evidence for considering empathy as a social skill. When we participate in psychodrama, our capacities for empathy are considerably extended. By using a training technique known as role reversal, Moreno is able to evoke dramatic insights. He views empathy as a two-way passage, punning on the difference between *Einfühlung* and *Zweifühlung*. In the dialogue both parties gain insight into each other: "A meeting of two: eye to eye, face to face. And when you are near I will take your eyes out and place them instead of mine, and you will take my eyes out and will place them instead of yours, then I will look at you with your eyes and you will look at me with mine" (1956, p. 6).

The psychodrama illustrates the function of the imagination in deepening empathic abilities under the stimulus of a contrived social situation. Here, the fantasy, unlike Mead's internal dialogue, does not remain entirely subjective nor is it necessarily rational and deliberate. In a sample situation, the role players change their identities and act as if they were other persons. A son takes the role of the father and the latter assumes the identity of the son. The *as-if* situation takes on dramatic intensity when a specific and emotionally charged issue is introduced. The participants improvise their own lines with only a minimum of cues, creating a character out of their own involvement and the unpredictable activity of their own fantasy. The drama is an *ersatz* life situation but the degree of involvement can be remarkably intense. The participants experience the same situation from more than one viewpoint, particularly when they are asked to switch roles. They have a keener appreciation of their similarity with each other. Those who vicariously participate in the psychodrama as members of an audience at a play find that their own role-playing ability is extended and their empathy sharpened.

It is important to analyze the structure of the psychodrama as an example of empathic role-taking in itself and as evidence of the correlation between empathic potential and social experience. Even those who are deficient in empathy to the point of being mentally ill are often able to recover or to gain greater flexibility in shifting roles. Moreno has empirically demonstrated that even the therapist's potential for empathy can be enhanced by training.

There is first a regressive factor. In this, as in all forms of play-acting, we express an innate impulse to imitate and to play without regard for appearances or fear of approval or disapproval. When we put on the mask of another role, we feel free to indulge our spontaneous fantasy. We lose our self-consciousness and surrender our attention and our energies to our imagination. There is a release from control and self-discipline as we come under the spell of a drama which emerges unpredictably out of the stimulus of the dramatic action. Feeling released from the inhibitions that are normal to his actual situation, the individual's imagination is spurred and he feels within himself echoes of a similarity and kinship that reach out to include an unusually wide variety of people. He plays with new identifications and tries out new roles with the abandon of the child he once was. Nothing really counts. The situation is a rehearsal, not the real thing. There are no penalties nor any loss of face. The imagination works more indulgently and more instinctively because the rational controls are lessened. There is no pressure to deal with reality or solve actual problems. When we are indifferent about our security and less concerned with conforming to stereotypes, the flow of our imagery is stronger. We see and hear with new vividness. We become alert to possible alternatives and we now can grasp intentions and meanings which in everyday experience we miss because of selective inattention.

Role-playing while regressive is actually capable of making us more objective in our insights into others. In a playful, unconcerned, and disinterested interaction with others, we see them as they actually are and not as we want or need them to be. We can become involved with them for what they are without having to make them over to suit our own needs. Our empathy becomes more genuine and less manipulative.

Another factor in role-playing, disposing us to more empathy, is the sense of similarity and group identification that derives from participating in a game with others. We become more open and suggestible as we recognize that we are members of the same in-group. With less need to manipulate the environment and to exploit our relationships with others, we see them without analyzing or evaluating them. There is a feeling of being connected and out of this a greater capacity for recognizing signs of similarity. There is still a mild anxiety about fulfilling a different kind or role. The role player is uncertain as to what others expect of him. He knows that it would be inappropriate for him to rely on his usual gestures and standard responses. But his tension is not so great as to make him fall back on his usual defensive tactics. It gives an edge to his performance because his feelings are aroused and he becomes engaged and involved. He is still free to indulge his fantasy and to respond spontaneously in roles that normally would seem quite foreign to him.

A variation of Moreno's psychodrama is the technique of fixed role therapy devised by George A. Kelley (1955). Here the participant improvises a new role or experiments with a different image of himself in actual life situations. He does not have the freedom of the actor in Moreno's theater, but even in his fixed role some of his dramatic and playful instincts are engaged more freely. The participant elicits new responses from his friends because of his own role revision. Then, reciprocally, he finds that he must respond in new ways to the changed expectations which others now have of him. He is wrenched out of his familiar context and under the challenge and stimulus of the new situation

finds that his own role-taking becomes more flexible. He discovers new dimensions in his own personality as well as in the
images he has of others.

Theodor Lipps and Aesthetic Empathy

Still another source for the study of the empathic skill can
be found in the more philosophic theories of empathy as a process
of aesthetic appreciation. The ideas of Theodor Lipps, who was
largely responsible for the introduction of the term *Einfühlung,*
of Vernon Lee, and of other writers on aesthetic theory have not
had a direct influence on psychology and psychiatry, but their
formulations of the way we empathically contemplate works
of art add substantially to our appreciation of psychological or
interpersonal empathy. We learn more of the cognitive function
of the emotions and the senses. We grasp the imaginative as well
as the motor or physical aspects of empathy. We learn to appreciate how empathic involvement and loss of self-consciousness
are achieved as we merge with the object we experience aestheti-
cally. Philosophers still debate the usefulness of empathy, one
group stressing the deeper grasp which involvement yields and
another arguing the need for "psychical detachment." A combination of the points of view of the "empathic" and the "detachment"
theories of aesthetics would be similar to the method of empathic
understanding described in Chapter II.

Lipps believed that empathy was a form of inner imitation.
An observer is stimulated by the sight of an object and responds
by imitating the object. The process is automatic and swift, and
soon the observer feels himself into the object, loses consciousness
of himself, and experiences the object as if his own identity had
disappeared and he had become the object himself. The observer
sees a mountain and apprehends it with his inner imaginative
activity, his muscles as well as with his eyes. As his gaze moves
upward to the peak of the mountain, his own neck muscles tense
and for the moment there is a sensation of rising. He is not aware
of the sensation, however. In describing the mountain he says that
it "rises." He experiences the mountain not as a static object

of great height but as an object which extends and rises from the valley to the clouds. It is not only an object but also a process or an activity. What the observer feels within himself (i.e., the sense of his own muscles stretching and his head lifting up), is a change or a movement which he instinctively applies to the mountain. Another illustration of the empathic tendency is found in the description of a segment of a line. We say that the line "extends" from point A to point B, as if the line did not exist on the paper as we first saw it but was actually engaged in moving between the two points. The activity of the eye in moving from the beginning to the end of the line is transposed on to the static drawing. We describe a large hall as "expansive," again reflecting an inner activity and projecting it on to an inanimate object. As we enter such a room, our chest may itself expand giving us a sensation of freedom and release. Without thinking of this inner activity as our own, we project it on to the room itself.

In addition to these common and relatively simple situations, we experience empathy when we project more complex emotional states. We discover our inner feelings about inspiration and beauty in external objects as if such spiritual qualities inhered in them. When we view the arches and lofty heights of a cathedral, we describe the structure as being "spiritual" and tend to believe that such qualities objectively belong to the structure itself. The specific combination of stone, line, and color becomes for us a tangible expression of beauty so that we apprehend the total structure as a *Gestalt* which is more meaningful to us. Without such empathy we would respond to details, observe dimensions, and notice the contrast of light and shadow without apprehending the edifice as an artistic whole.

These brief illustrations suffice for an overview of empathy in aesthetics. Obviously our survey cannot deal with specifically philosophic problems such as the reality of the external world and the possibility of any form of cognition. A related issue, which we do feel obliged to discuss (cf. below), is the nature of empathy as partly or completely projective. In psychology we are persuaded that empathy yields objective knowledge about subjects that are active and animated.

Lipps, for one, insisted that in artistic contemplation the subject enters into the object and is no longer conscious of the imitative activity of his muscles or his gestures. Since the activity is involuntary, his imagination dominates his entire being so that he is no longer conscious of the *as-if* activity. He becomes the object and is entirely identical with it. From one of the critics of the aesthetic theory of empathy has come a remarkably vivid and concise definition which is helpful to the layman in this difficult branch of philosophy:

Empathy means, if anything, to glide with one's own feeling into the dynamic structure of an object, a pillar, or a crystal or the branch of a tree, or even of an animal or a man, and as it were to trace it from within, understanding the formation and motoriality of the object with the perceptions of one's own muscles; it means to "transpose" oneself over there and in there (Buber, 1948, p. 97).

In the process the observer is stimulated by an external cue and responds by automatically and unconsciously associating the object with a familiar inner activity or sentiment, or attitude of his own. It is important to appreciate the fact that the similarity between the subject and the object existed before the moment of actual stimulation or excitation. Empathy is based on the principle of an *a priori* similarity. Our inner activity is a reservoir of feeling which is then tapped when we see a specific object. The linkage between this object and ourselves is instantaneous so that we spring from our own identity to the identity of the object. The activity within the self has its own fulfillment when it can be projected upon a concrete object and then experienced as something real. The sensations can be simple, like those of rising or expanding, or more complex and further removed from specific muscles, as in the case of sense-feelings like willing, power, and pride. The individual is carried away by his new identity. Lipps described a process of being released from all that we are and becoming entirely absorbed in the object of contemplation. Two of his statements are worth noting:

In esthetic imitation I become progressively less aware of muscular tensions or of sense-feelings in general the more I surrender in contemplation to the esthetic object.

Even spatially, if we can speak of the spatial extent of the ego,

I am in its place. I am transported into it. I am, so far as my consciousness is concerned, entirely and wholly identical with it (cf. Rader, 1935, pp. 298, 301).

How would such theories of aesthetic empathy account for "the empathy variable"? Two inferences might be drawn. First, beyond a certain minimum of sense-feelings commonly experienced, such as release from tension in entering a more spacious room or an experience of slow and graceful movement in observing a curved line, some individuals have poetic endowments and a vastly richer potential of impulses and sensitivities. Their reservoir of feeling and sensation would be deeper so that they might be expected to have a far more versatile empathic ability. Second, some individuals would be more suggestible and would receive a wider variety of cues from external objects. They might take in stimuli to which others, less sensitively endowed, would fail to respond. A symbol might trigger a standard reaction in many people, but a poet might project upon a flower a magnificent array of associations. Constitutional differences in sensory perception, sharpness and vividness of imagery, and animal vitality separate the amateur from the master. This point would be reinforced by the findings of modern psychology on innate differences in kinaesthetic, olefactory, auditory, and visual acuity.

Aesthetic theory distinguished, too, the degrees of emotional involvement of the same individual in different situations. We have the capacity of being lost in our work, or "absent in mind," like Archimedes running naked from his bath after making a discovery about hydraulics, or being so engrossed in drawing a figure in the sand that he did not observe the Roman with sword poised over head. Hypnotic absorption of such intensity is called "ecstatic." A second variation is the member of the audience in a theater who is a participant or *mitspieler,* taking the part of first one actor and then another. Still less intense is the absorption of the spectator. He is only superficially engaged by the scene he observes. He retains his own identity and experiences only a spasmodic and superficial similarity with the actors or the objects he views. Only empathy of the ecstatic kind would be genuine, according to Lipps.

The position of Martin Buber on ecstatic empathy, the state of being completely engrossed in the subject, is not as consistent. He rejects empathy because it means the dissolution of the self and prefers a process of "inclusion," a simultaneous experience of an event in terms of our own perspective and the perspective of another person. But in another connection he seems closer to Lipps. He protests any "division of consciousness": "If one is overcome by the emotion of anger as he tries to understand an angry man, he should allow this emotion to run its course without trying to gain a perspective" (Buber, 1948, pp. 125-126). After such total engagement or involvement, the empathizer can then recollect the event in his memory and consider its meaning from more than one viewpoint. In so far as Buber speaks of feeling fully and spontaneously in moments of experiencing the other side, he accepts the principle of a temporary loss of ego in ecstatic empathy. Mead also concurred in this thought, commenting that the living act is separate from reflective experience. The actor is completely caught up by his role and only after he has enacted a role in a particular situation can he catch it in his memory and then reflect upon what it means to him. *In situ*, the experience is completely subjective (Mead, 1934, p. 203).

We now need to account for the effectiveness of empathic appreciation. How does aesthetic theory explain the greater vividness and deeper penetration enjoyed by the empathic contemplator of external objects? One explanation has to do with the greater number of senses involved and the other, with the new insights that emerge out of the fusion of different sense impressions and out of the associations of the imagination. The stimulus of seeing or hearing an object releases a fantasy, setting off a chain reaction of images, some old but others new.

In abstract or disinterested observation, we use the sense of sight and avoid the other senses of smell, hearing, touch, and rhythm. If we examine Van Gogh's "Still Life with Onions," we consider the arrangement of the bottle, the plate of onions, the candle, and so on. We notice different colors and compare them with the colors in other paintings by this or other artists. But if we contemplate the same picture empathically, we are there, we smell the freshness of the green onions and touch their silky brown wrapping. Our palates taste both the wine and the onions. We hear the sound of the matchstick being grated against the box. Some observers with extremely projective empathy might feel themselves into the objects and sense their roundness and smoothness as the curves of their own muscles. In experiments on empathy with literary metaphors, Downey found that some subjects became the lizard described in Poe's line, "the swift and silent lizard of the stones," and felt themselves running around on their hands watching for enemies (1929, p. 188). Many experienced crawly feelings on reading the passage. In McKellar's investigation of the merging of the senses (synaesthesia), auditory stimuli like the notes of Bach were found to evoke tactile images as well (1957). Listeners not only heard the crisp tones but reported the sense of touching smooth, round, and shiny plastic objects. Such research findings document the aesthetic theory that inner experience is the more intense as different sensory impressions and associations merge. The object contemplated becomes more real or the person, in Buber's language, more "fully present."

Projection, Imagination, and Reality

Aesthetic theories of empathy help pinpoint some of the recurring issues in psychological or interpersonal empathy. These deal with the creative power of the imagination, as we have just seen, with the phenomenon of losing the self in contemplation, and with the question of the motor or more extrasensory character of empathic expression. Lipps did not offer an explanation in depth, as in psychoanalytic theory, of the ways in which we become totally absorbed in the identity of another. But his emphasis on the completeness of the absorption offers important insights. The phenomenon becomes understandable if we include the psychoanalytic insight of the unconscious "living" us. We are "lived" by other strata of our being as our ego becomes more passive and relaxed and we surrender to the involuntary activity of other levels of personality. Freud explained the *why* of the process, but it is to Lipps that we are indebted for a description of its pervasiveness and intensity.

To Lipps also we owe our appreciation of the empathic process as "spiritual" or imaginative rather than muscular or kinaesthetic. It is, as he insisted, "not a sensation in one's body, but feeling something, namely, oneself into the esthetic object." He believed that scientific esthetics had to recover from "this disease of preoccupation with sense-feelings." Like Lipps, a modern psychiatrist noted that empathy seems to baffle many observers because ". . . they cannot refer empathy to vision, hearing, or some other special sense receptor, and since they do not know whether it is transmitted by the ether waves or what not, they find it hard to accept the idea of empathy" (Sullivan, 1953, p. 41). Neither Lipps nor Sullivan accounted for the specific channels through which empathy is communicated, but both agree that the skill is not necessarily correlated with specific sense organs. It follows that Buber and other critics of the empathic theory are in error in identifying it only with sensual or kinaesthetic experience. Empathic or imaginative activity, according to another philosopher, involves the whole self:

"Imaginary" does not mean anything in the least like make-believe, nor does it imply that what goes by that name is private to the person who imagines. The "experience or activity" seems to be not sensuous, and not to be in any way specialized; it is some kind of general activity in which the whole self is involved (R. G. Collingwood, 1958, p. 152).

This emphasis on the "whole self" is most important since several sources make a distinction between actual emotion and empathy which is only "intellectual."

It is difficult for some persons to appreciate the fact that empathy involves feeling even if no specific sense organs undergo observable change because their thinking is still dominated by the James-Lange theory of the correlation of emotions and the body. But this theory, however popular, is by no means authoritative. The anthropologist Robert Briffault was one of several who challenged it, insisting that the theory accounted only for the grosser emotional states. Emotions like grief, anxiety, and aesthetic enjoyment can be experienced distinct from physical sensation (Briffault, 1921, p. 61). The same point was made by

Wolfgang Köhler. It is quite possible, he said, that our affective states are not necessarily related to the sense modalities. "No attempts to localize the neural substratum of a person's emotional states seem as yet to have passed beyond the stage of guess-work" (1959, p. 354).

Without pursuing further the general problem posed by the psychology of the emotions, we need only to observe that Lipps and other exponents of the nonsensory character of empathy have support in more recent theories of emotion. The argument that empathy is "intellectual" rather than emotional because it does not involve the body organs is therefore not tenable. It is worth noting, parenthetically, that the therapist using empathy as a trial identification does experience feeling, even though he is not physically agitated and is not conspicuously responding with his sensuous capacities.

Three possibilities exist: an empathizer has feelings along with somatic reactions; he has feelings with somatic reactions difficult to identify; he has feelings presumably without any somatic parallels. In any case there is genuine involvement. If we follow Lipps and Freud we would say that empathy does involve such realistic feeling. It may not, however, since we can visualize the feelings of others without necessarily sharing them. Such are the cases of novelists or actors who view their characters with personal detachment and who fail to become imaginatively and wholly identified with them. But when we empathize or participate fully and unreservedly, our emotions are evoked. Empathic feelings may be transient, as with the case of the therapist who identifies only long enough to get a "taste" of his patient's experience or just long enough to "get the picture." But for the moment, the emotions are real. Whether or not the empathizer must relate with love or with fellow-feeling, as Scheler would insist, is a problem we defer until Chapter V.

A major distinction between *aesthetic* and *interpersonal* empathy has to do with the similarity that the empathizer experiences. To what extent is empathy basically "projective"? To what extent does the empathizer experience feelings or attitudes that are objectively present in the other person? Obviously, aesthetic empathy is almost entirely projective. The inner activity of the observer is transposed into the inanimate object. The mountain does not "rise." The storm does not "rage." There may be some stimulation of a feeling of similarity as the observer perceives some cues in the object. The sight of a gently curving stream in the painting may lead the observer to feel himself moving from side to side. But if he takes the next step and imputes a sense of rhythm to the static design of form and color, he is obviously projecting his own inner states. Color may inhere in the painting, so some would argue, but the movement said to be in the painting is only a projection. There is no similarity to speak of between the human being who contemplates the painting and the canvas itself. If the painting happens to be a portrait of the observer himself, we still cannot speak of a similarity of emotional states between the subject and the portrait. The emotional state, whatever it might be, inheres only in the subject himself or in other persons who contemplate the painting.

This is, of course, not the case in psychological empathy where the empathizer already shares many points of similarity with the other person. He and his fellow are two of a kind. Moreover, the other person, unlike the inanimate object, possesses an emotional life which is actual and dynamic. Liveliness and emotionality do not have to be projected onto the other people. They have an inner activity of their own, even though, as in the case of the catatonic patient, it is elusive. Even allowing for the obvious distinction between an aesthetic object with no "existence" of its own and a human being, we must still deal with the issue of the projective character of empathy. Do we obtain objective knowledge of the feelings of the other person or do we merely attribute our own feelings to him, since we are naturally similar to him and our emotions are roughly parallel? The empathizer does not cease completely to be himself when he identifies. He may move from one ego state to another, but does he not still remain within himself and can he possibly communicate with another person whose existence is fundamentally separate from his own? Empathy ultimately is vicarious introspection—we introject the other person into ourselves and contemplate him inwardly. But we are still ourselves and it is our own imagination that is active, having been stimulated by the perceptual cues that came to us from the other person via our own eyes and our own ears.

Allowing for an absolute limitation on the degree to which it is possible for any one person to understand another or to communicate meanings and feelings, we can still say that empathy does provide us with objective knowledge. It is not projective, even though it is our own *a priori* similarity to our fellow that gives us a base from which to move in the direction of making this similarity more intense through empathizing. We are able to communicate with individuals who are different from us in significant degrees because we have enough in common to establish the first link and because we can vicariously experience those features of his own inner life that differ in degree from our own.

Certain realistic factors already surveyed account for this accretion of understanding. Darwin observed that when we imitate the other person's feeling, we arouse the same feeling in ourselves. Without such empathy or imitation, we would have a *conception* not an *experience* of the other person's feeling. Empathy also engages more of the personality, mental images become more varied and vivid, the perceiving activity is more intense, and the knowledge of the other person has the feel of actuality because it is more direct and more personal. An early source, quoted by W. J. Bates, accounts for the reality of empathic knowledge:

As we have no immediate experience of what other men feel, we can form no idea of the manner in which they are affected, but by conceiving what we ourselves should feel in like situation. Though our brother is on the rack, as long as we ourselves are at our ease, our senses will never inform us of what he suffers. They never did and never can carry us beyond our persons, and it is by the imagination that we can form any conception of what are his sensations (Adam Smith, 1759, quoted in Bates, 1956, pp. 134-135).

Finally, we recall that empirical investigations by Moreno and others indicate that significant improvements do occur in our understanding of others after empathic experiences. In some degree it is possible to check the validity of our insights by examining the responses of the subject to the empathizer. Comparing the outsider's view of the feelings of the subject with the subject's own estimate of his feelings is never a scientific operation of any precision, but it is reliable enough to serve as a basis for evaluating the empathic skill. Research in social psychology indicates that the empathic skill is functional and often accurate.

Summary

The following chart provides an overview of the different ways a number of disciplines approach the so-called mystery of the empathic skill. The theme of similarity is the unifying motif among these theories. All attempt to account for the way in which we communicate by participating in similar or identical experiences. Ultimately these are techniques for reducing social distance and achieving what the sociologists have defined as in-group empathy. If we comprehend those whom we resemble, how do we achieve (or reinstate) this essential resemblance? From this chart we also gain a perspective on such recurring issues as the destiny of the empathic skill in the individual as it atrophies, becomes stabilized, or becomes more effective. It helps us to appreciate the relative impact of instinct and learning on the emergence of empathy.

It is obvious that those disciplines dealing with the instinctual endowment of man would tend to think of empathy as a primitive skill capable of being atrophied by the process of culture. The point of view represented by the social psychologists (both Mead and Moreno) allows for the growth and enhancement of empathic skill through social experience and training. Psychoanalytic theory is located between the biological and the more sociological disciplines and sees empathy as partly instinctual and partly learned. The most rationalistic conception of empathy was advanced by Mead. He saw it more as a skill in communication of ideas than as a sensing of diffuse emotional states in the other person. In the theories of Lipps we noted the significant emphasis on the completeness of the similarity or the identification. It is not a focused, specialized act of communication but a state of being in which the subject participates so extensively and deeply that his own ego is submerged in the object he contemplates.

	Origins The Empathy Variable	Channels Muscular-Kinaesthetic and/or Imaginative
Biology	Similarity of structure is given. Nonverbal cues elicit same responses. Primordial empathy derives from participation in original and common existence.	Endowment of impulses similar in members of same species. Instinct for imitation and play. Innate tendency to affiliate and participate in group life. Sympathetic vibration of musculatures.
Freud	Partly instinctual, partly cultural. Cannibalistic impulse surviving in introjection. Imitative impulse. Identification as defense mechanism against internal and external threats.	An activity of the psyche. Overt only in hysterical forms. Shifting of selves or ego states, permeability of boundaries between conscious and unconscious. Suggests the idea of a collective or group ego as deep layer of the unconscious.
Mead	A skill in dealing with verbal symbols and cues acquired in interaction with others. Function of experience. Self a precipitate of the social process.	Largely internal. Imaginative and intellectual-rational skill for internal dialogue with others. A secondary process.
Moreno	Assumes existence of an affiliative need. Endowment of spontaneous impulsive activity. Subject to evocation through social interaction.	Basically an as-if activity of the imagination. Muscular-kinaesthetic imitation stimulates empathy.
Lipps	Individual has innate structure of drives and activities. Is sensitive or suggestible. Instinctively feels similarity and follows play instinct.	Not a matter of sense feeling but activity of the imagination in which individual is fused with object contemplated. Unconscious projection of self into object.

The empathic skill is exercised when the subject is stimulated by another person. The stimulus may be actual and overt as in a personal encounter or more symbolic as in reading a description of a person or a situation. It is necessarily a stimulus of a concrete, specific kind to which the body and/or the psyche of the subject responds spontaneously. Empathy may take the form of a vibration or a parallel activity of the sense organs or an imaginative reconstruction of the other person's behavior or emotional states. When it is imaginative, it is an unconscious activity in which the subject experiences a variety of images which cannot be correlated with specific sense organs. He is seized, as it were, by emotional states that are similar to those of the person with whom he empathizes. He has a sense of being connected to the other person, of participating in his experience with a temporary loss of self-consciousness, and of relaxation of his own focus of attention. Into his empathic response enter his previous social experience, traces of his preverbal existence, memories of an original group membership as well as of a sense of belonging in a common ego. The empathic skill may be both reactive and regressive as well as adaptive and experimental. It seems mysterious because it expresses nonrational and nonverbal capacities for communication. These may be an expression of innate dramatic and imaginative powers. They may also reflect an instinct common to the species for recognizing nonverbal cues and gestures. The sense of directness and immediacy of communication derives from the dramatic quality of empathy in which one person seems to participate in the inner life of another and also from the automatic nature of the skill of recognizing nonverbal cues, bypassing, as it does, the more elaborate processes of communication via linguistic symbols arranged in logical sequence.

The empathic activity itself is almost entirely an intrapsychic process. It takes place concurrently with shifts in ego states and with alternating states of consciousness. It is motivated by the human need to communicate, to share in the emotions of others, to affiliate and overcome loneliness, to recover lost ties, and to apprehend by techniques of dramatic imagination. These needs are not in conflict with others that are also cognitive. Empathy simply engages more parts of the personality. It yields the *how* and the *what* of human understanding.

IV

USES FOR PRACTITIONER
AND CLIENT

WE INTEND this chapter to link the earlier chapters dealing more generally with the theories of empathy to the remaining chapters which will deal with variables bearing on the successful practice of empathy by counselors and therapists. What particular insights into the nature of empathy have specific relevance for the task of the counselor and the therapist? In what ways are diagnostic competence and therapeutic effectiveness determined by the components of the empathic skill? What are the possibilities for enhancing professional skills and what, from the other side, are the blocks and errors that are commonly experienced in faulty communication? We shall develop more fully the observation made in our first chapter concerning the double role of empathy as an experience of everyman and as a professional tool of the helper in human relations. We shall also have to come to grips again with the ambiguity of the term "empathy." Is it a kind of inside knowledge of the other person, a matter of content or a process leading to such content, a form of relating or of knowing, or a combination of all of these elements?

Some cross reference will be made to the theories of the empathic skill which we outlined in the preceding chapter. Although it is important to appreciate the full range of forces and situations which have a bearing on a theoretical understanding of empathy, we shall not find an immediate and specific correlation between the actual work of the therapist and each aspect of these theories.

In the present chapter we shall largely be concerned with internal psychological processes, their dynamics, and the purposes they serve with respect to the practitioner and the client. We find especially relevant the concepts of identification as defined by Freud and the processes of role-taking as described by Mead and Moreno. Since we want to explore the living and fluid relationship that takes place in the interview, we have less concern now with Lipps and the aesthetic theories that are concerned in the main with only one kind of projection—the inner activity of the observer or the artist experiencing objects rather than people. The biological factors we reviewed alert us to the possibility that the empathies of both the professional and the client may be more dependent than we realize on innate or constitutional differences in sensitivity to the cues and responses of others. We cannot avoid wondering about the fate of such raw and instinctive empathy as the maturing individual comes to rely less on sensuous capacities, inhibits his spontaneity, and almost one-sidedly develops his intellectual and secondary processes. Questions about the channels of empathy will still remain but we shall deal with empathy as a psychological rather than a muscular or kinaesthetic response. The problem of whether empathy is "real" or "imaginative" will again confront us in Chapter V when we turn to the issues of the actual feelings of the counselor-therapist for the client and when we try to clarify what we mean when we say that he "participates" in the experience of the other.

We gain a deeper knowledge of empathy as a phenomenon

in itself, if we now focus our attention on the interview. It offers us a richer field of study than the empathic interaction of the actor and his audience. There is a continuous dialogue between the professional and his client. It flows back and forth, taking new forms and expressing itself with greater flexibility and variety. The interview is an excellent laboratory and the records of empathic communication between therapist and client have been subjected to a continuous and concentrated study by specialists in psychological processes. We can find, certainly, finer descriptions of empathic responses in the writings of the dramatists and the poets. Psychologists from Freud to the present can only bow in admiration before Shakespeare's power of empathic description so keenly revealed in Hamlet's protest to Rosencrantz and Guildenstern:

You would play upon me; you would seem to know my stops; you would pluck out the heart of my mystery; you would sound me from my lowest note to the top of my compass; and there is much music, excellent voice in this little organ; yet you cannot make it speak. 'Sblood, do you think I am easier to be played on than a pipe? Call me what instrument you will, though you can fret me, you cannot play upon me   (Act III, ii).   (Freud, 1953, p. 262.)

It is a question not of finding descriptions that are both subtle and vivid but of systematic analysis of the components of empathy. Only a few therapists can write so vividly about empathic experiences with clients in the manner of a Theodor Reik. However, many have been able to reflect on their own experiences and to record for us a number of valuable insights into the nature and operation of empathy. Their self-studies and reports of their patients are more relevant to our research interests than the more statistical type of empirical research done by specialists in social psychology and sociometry. A number of research projects have been concerned with measuring socioempathy among members of age or status groups but afford less insight into the nature of the empathic process. They deal with personal preferences, social distance, and recognition of specific cues and do not attempt to deal in depth with more intensive and subtle empathic interactions.

The same lack of focus on the individual and the fuller range of private experience is found in the interview of the anthropologist engaged in pure research. He takes care not to disturb or change the culture of the group he is studying. He is usually concerned with empathy as a technique of cognition, not as a force for change. It could distract him from his essential purpose if it were to call for a continuous personal involvement or for the establishment of an intimate personal relationship designed to create psychological changes in his subject. He is less concerned than the therapist with the study of the individual *per se*, because he cultivates the individual subject as a prototype of the culture-group.

The therapist, committed to helping or changing his client or patient, is particularly interested in what is personal and subjective and therefore focuses his attention on all that concerns the problems and needs of the specific individual who has requested his help. His empathy, being more intense and penetrating, offers us our richest research leads. (To be sure, social scientists sometimes succeed in getting inside information which escapes therapists. Sociologists disguised as patients have experienced the culture of mental hospitals from within and have uncovered unusual data about particular attitudes of patients as well as about the group.) Since the therapist's personal involvement is greater, his empathic experiences have deeper dimensions. He responds to patients who are motivated by a greater variety of needs and more urgent emotions than are the subjects usually chosen for anthropological study. Moreover, if psychoanalytically oriented, he has trained himself to study and interpret his subjective responses. He knows that his own feelings or empathic responses serve at least two functions: they are indices of the feelings of the patient and, at the same time, subtle forces bearing on the course of the therapy itself.

Empathic Skills—for Professional and for Client

In Chapter I we noted that empathy is a common human experience as well as a professional tool of the specialist. It is interesting to compare the empathic skills in more detail from the standpoints of both the therapist and the client. Proficiency in empathy is a criterion useful in distinguishing between the individual who needs therapy and the individual whose mental or emotional health is adequate and who neither seeks nor requires psychological assistance. The progress of a client or patient can often be measured in terms of an increase in a capacity for empathy.

If empathy is a variable among the so-called normal individuals and among clients for psychological help, it is at the same time a kind of variable among therapists. Even though it is an important variable and one that we intend to emphasize, it is not the only one. Diagnostic knowledge, skill in observation, clinical experience, and many other factors enter into the preparation of the effective counselor or therapist. Some therapeutic specialists emphasize the somatic processes, others the psychological, and still others the social. Many are eclectic in their approach. Psychoanalysis, for example, has many subgroups with particular therapeutic orientations but in general is characteristically attentive to instinctual and unconscious processes. Casework is perhaps distinctive with its emphasis on interpersonal processes. Without surveying the considerable variety of counseling and therapeutic roles, it is obvious that many different skills help determine the effectiveness of the professional, and each profession obviously establishes certain standards of its own. It would be easy to oversimplify their range and variety. The main concern of this study is with the empathic variable itself, which is relevant to all counseling roles. Too often it is taken for granted. The potentialities of this subjective process in the counselor or therapist are not sufficiently cultivated. This impression is held without respect to the particular therapeutic specialty.

The therapist's moments of greater effectiveness, both as diagnostician and as healer, have a positive correlation with his empathic capacities. Some of the deficiencies and blocks in empathy that limit his effectiveness in his role tend, in more exaggerated and intensive forms, to make for handicaps and emotional problems in the everyday experience of the client. In the former case, it is a question of skillfully performing professional responsibilities for his client. In the case of the layman or the client, it is a question of failing to establish or to maintain communication with others. The gifted therapist can feel his way into the inner world of a client. The healthy individual gets the viewpoint of the other person concerning himself and takes the viewpoint of others so that he can anticipate their behavior.

Both professional and client require the same capacity for being in touch with one's own inner experience and for being in touch with the inner experience of others. What distinguishes the therapist from the ordinary layman in matters of empathic communication is the degree of sensitivity, the ability to control one's own responses, and the resourcefulness and energy necessary for communicating when unusual stresses and distortions intrude. The psychological information the therapist must acquire as part of his preparation for his profession is technical and sophisticated, nearly always beyond the reach of the amateur and usually remote from his needs or interests. But the empathic skill of the practitioner, as distinguished from his clinical knowledge and his training in diagnosis, is something that he shares, in degree, with everyman. It is only when we think of empathic understanding as a process of involvement and detachment (Chapter II) do we realize how much special competence and virtuosity the therapist adds to the empathic skill that we might reasonably expect to find in the normal or healthy layman.

In his nonprofessional role, the therapist uses no more empathy than might be expected of any man who communicates with relatives, friends, or associates. When he accepts the responsibilities of counseling or therapy, he draws on his specialized training in empathic skills. He must demonstrate more than ordinary empathy, for his success as a practitioner depends on his ability to attune to higher frequencies than are required in normal, everyday reception. It should be noted that the nonprofessional is likewise expected to respond with unusual empathy when members of his own family turn to him for support or in other emergencies when he takes the role of helper. While empathic ability of a high order is often found in laymen, it is more common among artists and professional interviewers.

The importance of the empathy variable for the therapist has been underscored by the late Frieda Fromm-Reichmann. She observed that in the early days of psychoanalytic therapy the personality of the particular therapist was not considered to be a significant variable. All that were important were training, integrity, and medical responsibility. More attention is now given to the empathic relationship. "We know now that the success or failure of psychoanalytic therapy is, in addition, greatly dependent upon the question of whether or not there is an empathic quality between the psychiatrist and the patient" (1950, p. 62).

A contemporary psychoanalyst, Leslie Farber, makes the same point in an interesting way, when he observes that something beyond the question of technical competence enters into the judgment which one therapist makes of his colleagues when he must refer a friend or relative for treatment. He becomes concerned with the possibility of "meeting" or of empathic communion which may be more likely in the case of therapist A than with therapist B or C. "But as our concern for his fate increases, we abandon our technological rules and ask instead, What manner of human being will deal with our friend's distress?" (1957, p. 22).

The following chart, which restates some of the earlier materials on "empathic skill" and "empathic understanding," clarifies some of the uses of empathy that are common to the client and the therapist. At the same time the chart helps us appreciate the distinctive and specialized uses of empathy by the professional practitioner.

This chart anticipates certain implications that are soon to be discussed more fully. We shall, for example, review the circumstances which lead the client to become deficient in the minimum amount of empathy he needs. Often it is a question of degree of intensity and proficiency that distinguishes the professional and the client in their respective use of empathy. For his recovery, the client requires a definite enhancement of his empathic skills. The therapist, for adequacy in his role of helper, requires a higher and more technical competence in the same skills. Far more is required of him as a professional with respect to the use of empathy and the engagement of his powers of comprehending and relating subjectively than would be either

Empathic Skill	Client	Therapist
Constitutional, innate *biological sensitivity* to similarity with others and recognition of cues.	Needs minimum ability; some atrophy of ability as he conforms to social patterns and inhibits instinctive responses.	Tries to maximize this skill; overconformity and one-sided development of secondary or rational processes a handicap to the fullest communication with client.
To participate in group and enjoy empathy with members of same in-group.	Necessary for understanding and sense of belonging, as in family, work-group.	Requires ability to establish new in-group with his client, to share his world and establish supportive relationship only as long as therapy is in progress; a temporary and somewhat artificial group.
To identify a. As defense mechanism.	a. Appropriate in childhood but source of distortion in adult.	a. Deterrent to therapeutic roles.
b. As technique for understanding.	b. Necessary for everyday communication.	b. Greater degree necessary in order to gain knowledge of internal frames of reference when verbal communication is inadequate.
c. As way of gaining sense of relatedness and emotional participation in life of other.	c. Source of emotional support and status essential for healthy self-esteem.	c. The achieved sense of relatedness not for security needs of therapist but for establishing the sense of being understood and appreciated which the client anticipates.

Empathic Skill	Client	Therapist
To take role of other a. In Mead's sense of experiencing inwardly the same meaning of the symbols and words addressed to the other or received from him.	a. Minimum of competence necessary for communication.	a. Higher degree of competence so that subtle and idiosyncratic meanings can be comprehended. Special concern with client's private language and imagery.
b. In Moreno's sense, to take the social role or occupy the psychological space of another.	b. A minimum ability in order to anticipate behavior or needs of intimates and associates and gain feed-back on appropriateness of one's own feelings or intended social acts.	b. May use psychodrama as therapeutic technique. Requires flexibility in imaginary role-taking, professional concern with client's interpersonal and situational roles.
To be emotionally labile; to enjoy motility in psychological states.	A minimum of inner flexibility is necessary to facilitate communication with others and to touch different parts of one's own inner experience and overcome shallowness of affect.	Greater need to be able to regress and draw on more primary techniques of communication. Need to draw on wider range of inner experience. Need to become involved emotionally with variety of patients and with changing moods of specific patient.
To control or modify excessive or deficient empathy.	Extremes in either direction and lack of a reasonable range of mood swing are indices of disturbance and illness.	Requires more than usual empathic ability as well as greater powers of control and detachment.

necessary or appropriate in his private or nonprofessional roles. Were he to carry over into his private life the empathic skills he uses with his clients, he would convert his home into a clinic and betray a deficiency in empathy as regards what is appropriate to the roles of husband, father, or group member. At the same time, the client, like the professional in his private life, has need of no more empathic skill than is required for effective communication, for realistic and appropriate behavior, and for spontaneous participation in the familial, social, and occupational groups to which he belongs. He could, of course, cultivate his empathic skills beyond what is needed for his emotional health or for his roles as relative or friend. Were he to do more, he would likely have the intention of becoming a professional practitioner of empathy, as artist, therapist, or conceivably, as a manipulator of one kind or another, or as an expert in thought-reform.

A chart indicating the relative concern of the practitioner and client with the four phases in the process of empathic understanding (Chapter II, pp. 38ff.) seems unnecessary. We have emphasized the fact that the therapist uses empathic skills as part of a larger process of cognition and of therapy. He learns to oscillate between merger and detachment. He combines clinical knowledge and dispassionate analysis with emotional involvement. He puts his experience of the other person and his own experience of himself to ingenious and creative uses. If he is psychoanalytically oriented, he cultivates his own unconscious and empathizes on deep levels with himself and with others. Such refined and technical uses of empathic understanding are not relevant to the client nor are they within his reach without specialized training. Unlike the therapist, he does not have to disengage himself so objectively from the groups in which he participates. At crucial junctures in the course of family life, he may put forth the unusual energy required for deeper empathic communication. Most of his relationships are casual and superficial and do not require getting to the depths of feeling in others. The therapist, however, regularly confronts emergency situations in the lives of his clients and deep empathy in his professional role is by no means exceptional. He may succeed in varying degrees, but he is accustomed to communicate at the deeper levels and to put forth the energy which is necessary for penetrating superficial exchanges or rationalizations for actual intentions or emotions. He must constantly refine his understanding so that each effort brings him closer to what his client tries to express as well as to what his client tries to conceal.

While we have emphasized the greater competence of the therapist in the use of empathic skills and have noted the particular relevance of high empathy for the counseling roles, we need to recall that a number of variables determine the course of empathy so that at times a client or a layman may achieve greater empathy than the professional. It is conceivable that a husband might understand his wife with more empathy than his wife's therapist. A friend might communicate where the professional could fail completely. However, unless the layman or client is an individual of rare empathic powers, his successful communication is generated by the particular relationship that already exists between himself and the other person. It is not a versatile talent. On the other hand, professionals usually achieve considerable empathy with a diversity of clients, even though it is still true that a given therapist is often more empathic with one client than with another and may even experience different degrees of empathy from one hour to another in his relationship with the same client.

For their professional competence therapists must develop empathy of an intense kind with numbers of individuals who are, initially at least, complete strangers to them. They require talent for inviting intimacy, for relieving fears, and for evoking trust. The demands for empathic responses in everyday relationships in the case of the client are less strenuous because he finds himself associating with individuals who themselves have at least conventional empathic powers and because he has had repeated experiences in common with the same friends or co-workers. Standardized messages will do well enough.

Low Empathy and the Motivation for Therapy

Before considering empathy as a diagnostic category used by the psychologist and the therapist, we briefly note the inner experience of the low empathizer.

There are varying degrees of empathic deficiency and varying personal responses to the role of low empathizer. By no means are individuals necessarily aware of the level of their empathy nor are those who experience the consequences of such deficiency always motivated to seek help. Some personality types do not find their failures in empathy to be ego-alien or dissatisfying. The narcissist who is preoccupied with himself may not be even remotely interested in enhancing his sensitivity to others. The severely regressed schizophrenic who does not distinguish between himself and the outside world and is cut off from social experience no longer experiences any need to make changes in his system of communication. The criminal or sociopathic personality is an example of an individual with greatly distorted empathy who has no concern with improving his capacity to identify sensitively with others. He has few if any problems of conscience and has no insight into the errors he makes when he projects onto others the negative feelings he has about himself or when he fails completely to relate to his victim as anything more than an object.

The potential client, unlike the narcissist, the schizophrenic, or the sociopath, recognizes that something is wrong. He may not be able to diagnose his own difficulties in terms of deficiency in empathy or conceptualize his problems of communication, but he experiences the consequences of empathic failures and the bewilderment and discomfort he feels motivate him to seek help. One client may look for guidance in improving his communication with his employer. Another will consult a family therapist in order to re-establish empathy with a marriage partner. A depressed or anxious individual will turn for psychological assistance in order to overcome the sense of isolation or of personal worthlessness. Still others will seek psychotherapy because of a fear of losing their minds; they are frightened by their growing inability to think clearly and to make objective judgments. Even those who come to physicians for the relief of physical symptoms and for the treatment of organic illnesses are often found to have deficiencies in empathy. Their illnesses are linked with conflicts in communication, with repressions of attitudes and feelings, with disassociations among the parts of their personality. While the psychological components of his ailment may become apparent to the doctor long before they do to the patient himself, and while it is true that it was the symptom which motivated him to seek help originally, it is also true that the symptom may prove to be a symbol pointing to empathic failures.

The complaints of individuals who are candidates for psychological help have some connection with problems in effective empathy. Often the actual step toward therapy is not taken until the individual is seriously challenged by some new situation or emergency that requires greater empathic powers. He finds himself pressed to understand new situations and new role expectations or to redefine relationships which he may have outgrown or which have been interrupted by factors over which he has no control. When the demands are too great for his empathic capacity, he may turn for help in modifying his own reactions or for insight into his needs.

Everyone living in a mobile, mass society must be able to make rapid adjustments in attitude and to maintain self-esteem in the face of many threats. The poor empathizer is simply more vulnerable than the average citizen. He is less qualified to cope with conflicts and is less defended against the anxieties of living in a society of increasing alienation. In sum, he lacks the empathic ability which Daniel Lerner has described as "a basic personality skill in sorting one's stock of identities that equips man for continuous rearrangement of his self-system" (1959, p. 10).

What does it mean when one must live with empathies that prove unreliable, superficial, and dissatisfying? What are the characteristics of the poor empathizer as seen from within?

He finds it difficult to communicate both ideas and feelings. He misses the feedback of the data he needs to assess his own behavior and lacks the sense of mutuality which he requires in order to maintain his self-esteem. The judgments he makes of others are out of harmony with the judgments of other group members or associates. He tends to misconstrue the attitudes of others at the same time that he feels others do not respond to him in ways that he would consider appropriate or satisfactory. On the one hand he is frustrated in attempting to manipulate reality and in making appropriate decisions. On the other hand he experiences a degree of strangeness or alienation in his affective relationships with others. He has no secure sense of belonging to the group and feels deprived of the support and security of group empathy. He experiences himself too in a more detached and unsatisfactory way. He is disassociated from himself as well as from others. As he fails to contact others in a meaningful and sensitive way, so he fails to sustain an inner sense of integration and self-acceptance. To use Martin Buber's somewhat unusual but at the same time persuasive and useful term, the individual relates to others and to himself in "I-It" rather than "I-Thou" relationships. People become objects rather than fellow human beings; he becomes an object to himself. He suffers from a lack of stable identity and feelings of anxiety because of an inability to experience himself as alive, genuine, and spontaneous. The greater the degree of empathic deficiency the greater the sense of alienation from others and from oneself.

The failure to communicate and to relate to others which inevitably is linked with a sense of inner alienation leads to anxiety. Even if the individual unconsciously attempts to defend himself against this anxiety and does not experience it for what it is, he feels insecure and dissatisfied. If he is able to taste some of his own anxiety, he will experience it as a sign of his loneliness and isolation. Unable to communicate with others or to commune with himself, he senses an inner discomfort. A need that is basic to his existence is not being met adequately. He becomes lonely for others and for himself. Even if he is able to attend to the more routine responsibilities of living without interruption, as is the case of the mildly neurotic individual, he experiences a sense of despair at one level of his being or another. His needs for intimacy, for response, and for acceptance go unmet. When the sense of isolation becomes intolerable and the experience of disorientation from reality is too painful, the individual may be driven to psychosis. When the client's sense of reality is more or less intact, it is more difficult for the outsider to sense the consequences of his deficiency in empathy.

For the client himself the sense of frustration and perplexity is both real and acute. He may not grasp the genesis of his difficulties, but his experience of himself and his relationships with others are not gratifying. When and if he presents himself to a helper, he may feel desperate about his situation and have little confidence that he can be helped. He may, on the other hand, expect a magic cure or transformation. Each to his own, the individual client has some hope that he can re-establish or strengthen his relationships with others and that he can experience himself as a more productive and acceptable person. His deficiencies in empathy (among other problems) bring him to the therapeutic relationship. If his therapist can empathize with him, he in turn can empathize first with the therapist and ultimately with people in his normal environment and with himself. He requires a heightening of his own empathic capacities. His needs will be met when his helper proves to be an effective practitioner of empathic understanding.

Empathy and Standards of Positive Mental Health

Psychologists and therapists find that the empathy variable in potential clients is useful as a diagnostic category. Almost every model of the healthy personality includes some reference to the capacity to communicate and to establish sensitive personal relationships. It is an *a priori* assumption that empathy, as cognition and as affective state, is correlated with psychological well-being. Degrees of ill health can therefore be identified as variations in the degree of empathic capacity, ranging from minor insensitivities to gross distortions. Most frames of reference include both the cognitive and the affective components of the empathic skill, although competence in understanding the symbols and associations of others is often stressed more than the capacity to give and to receive the emotional responses which make empathic relationships possible.

The psychologically healthy individual developed as he did because he made a series of successful identifications. He learned how to participate in the feelings of others. His subjective needs for love and acceptance were met at the same time that he learned through identifying and role-taking to gain objective knowledge about others and about himself. In describing him as having ego-strength, we would say that he can empathize with himself in the sense of being able to objectify his own experiences. In the terms of social psychologists like George H. Mead, the healthy individual is able to arouse in himself the kind of response that his words arouse in others. He incorporates within himself the role-expectations of others. In Freud's thinking, mental health was linked with the capacity for enjoyment and achievement in life and involved the channeling and investment of one's emotional energies. Interpreting his position in the light of a capacity for empathy, we can see that he stressed the ability to muster and to distribute properly the emotional energy required for empathic relationships. In his words, "A strong egoism is a protection against falling ill, but in the last resort, we must begin to love in order not to fall ill, and we are bound to fall ill if, in consequence of frustration, we are unable to love" (1957a, p. 85).

Erich Fromm has made the same point. He moves from a recognition of the role of love or empathic sensitivity in mental health to a statement of therapeutic philosophy: "Analytic therapy is essentially an attempt to help the patient gain or regain his capacity for love" (1950, p. 87).

It is Fromm who helps us appreciate the close association between empathy as successful *cognition* and empathy as a sensitive *relationship*. His concept of "productive thinking" provides us with a way of conceptualizing the two functions of the empathic skill and of grasping their inner connections. The healthy individual is able to do more than exercise a power of intelligence useful in manipulating objects and obtaining routine information. He is distinguished by a capacity for reason which enables him to understand profoundly.

to know, to understand, to grasp, to relate oneself to things by comprehending them. It penetrates through the surface of things in order
to discover their essence, their hidden relationships and deeper
meanings, their "reason" (1947, pp. 102-103).

Disturbances in the power of productive thinking can be seen as
being at one and the same time deficiencies in cognition and
failures in establishing sensitive relationships.

The healthy individual has the capacity for objective understanding, both of others and of himself and enjoys the sense of
psychological security that comes from such accurate and reliable
knowledge. At the same time his subjective needs for giving love
to others and for receiving acceptance from them are adequately
met. He has a sense of relatedness to himself and to others and
enjoys the gratifications of self-respect and of the respect and
intimacy he recognizes that others feel for him. His psychological
equilibrium is maintained through the full exercise of his empathic capacities.

If we use empathy as a diagnostic category, we can distinguish
degrees of emotional maladjustment or mental illness as variations
in the exercise of empathic skills. It also helps us, as we are soon
to observe, to formulate the goals of therapy. We shall see too
that it is the therapist's own empathic powers which help to
evoke and to strengthen the client's empathy and assist his psychological recovery or readjustment.

What does the diagnostician or the therapist find in the case
of the candidate for therapy? He can, of course, formulate in
sophisticated psychological terms the kind of inner experience
which we previously described from the point of view of the
client himself. The poor empathizer is the individual who cannot see himself objectively (that is, see himself as others see him).
His orientation toward reality is therefore distorted. He has little
ability for *as-if* behavior, being unable to experiment with his
own reaction patterns and unable to take the perspective which
others may use. His emotional energies are bound up with maintaining a stereotyped image of himself and of others. He is prone
to all kinds of errors about himself and others. Since he lacks empathic ability, as Rosalind F. Dymond has observed, he has little
insight and no solid basis for his self-esteem:

In these cases the individual does not project himself into the thoughts and feelings of the other and so does not arrive at a self other pattern which is well rounded and which corresponds well with the actual relationship. He builds instead a meager or false representation of the relationship and lacks insight into the fact that he has done this (1948, p. 228).

He is disoriented to the degree that he does not *experience* or *feel* what he understands or what he presumes he understands correctly.

The sensitivities of the client are underdeveloped in some cases and overdeveloped in others. He may suffer from a deficiency in empathy or, possibly, an exaggerated or excessive empathy which blocks him from appreciating his sense of individuality and differentness. Some individuals, both healthy and disturbed, have a capacity for empathic eavesdropping, to use Frieda Fromm-Reichmann's terminology. They have an unusual talent for identifying the inner states of others and of grasping their hidden attitudes or intentions. The skill in nonverbal communication which some schizophrenics demonstrate appears puzzling and almost uncanny, but is actually quite limited and unrewarding. What they cannot do is extend such fragmentary and transitory insights over a period of time or, even more significantly, interpret their impressions and respond to them appropriately. Individuals who experience psychotic breaks with reality can be seen as exhibiting in more intense and severe forms the consequences of the same empathic deficiency which marks the neurotic or the mildly troubled individual. What so often lies at the core of emotional difficulty is a disturbance in empathy which takes the form of rigidity in thinking and feeling. In Norman Cameron's words, "This fixity of perspective, which is so characteristic of nearly all delusions, is what psychiatrists mean when they say that a patient lacks insight. He sees things only from a single standpoint for which he seems unable to substitute any other, even for the purpose of the moment" (1947, p. 94).

How do we account for the failure of some individuals to develop adequate empathy, for their deficiency in taking the roles of others, for identifying with their feelings, and for establishing the empathic relationships essential for positive mental health? It must be true that some individuals suffer from an impoverished constitution; their empathic deficiency is built-in. Another determining factor is the quality of early relationships. The poor empathizer may come from a family which was cold and unaccepting. At an early stage of his emotional development, his needs for emotional response were not gratified so that he developed a sense of deprivation or an insatiable hunger for affection. His need for love may have become so exaggerated that reality was never capable of meeting his expectations. If he learned to repress his needs, he paid the price of a lack of spontaneity and responsiveness, which added to his original sense of frustration and loneliness. He may have developed a skill for empathic communication, but the data his skill returned to him may have been so negative as to generate a sense of his own worthlessness. If empathy is a skill which can be described as "a process by which the infant discovers the reference points which help determine his emotional attitude toward himself" (Rioch, 1949, pp. 83-84), much of his subsequent mental health would be affected by the kind of feedback on himself that he absorbed early in life either consciously or unconsciously.

When Professionals Use Empathy

Our perspective now shifts from the empathic needs of the client to the professional practice of the counselor or therapist and the ways in which he uses his own empathic capacities to become more effective as a healer and psychological resource.

The subject of the professional use of empathy was introduced in Chapter I and reference was made in a general way to the advantages of achieving a sense of similarity or identity with the client. What we are now concerned with is the exploration in greater depth of the functions of such professional empathic activities. We know that empathy is used both as a technique for comprehending the client and as a relationship which in itself is therapeutic. However, it is necessary that we understand some of the points of agreement and disagreement among different therapists and in different schools of psychological theory regarding the following issues:

1. The relative effectiveness in therapy of insights gained by the therapist and conveyed to the client by means of empathy and the quality of the empathic relationship itself.
2. The relative degree to which the therapist reveals or communicates his feelings to the client.
3. The depth and range of the therapist's empathy with the client —the relative emphasis on empathizing with conscious and less conscious levels in the client's personality.

From such a comparative study may emerge a more sensitive appreciation of the potential contributions of empathic processes to effective therapy. Not all therapists use empathy for the same reasons or at the same depth, and there is no complete agreement on the advantages in therapy itself of a shared empathic relationship between professional and client. Much depends on treatment goals, on theories concerning the origin of emotional problems, and convictions about the curative power of insight. It is our impression that, regardless of whether cognition or therapy is emphasized, therapists do not cultivate their own empathic powers as sensitively and as ingeniously as they might. Our discussion of the uses of empathy crosses the lines that distinguish one professional group from another and does not confine itself to a single viewpoint among various psychoanalytic schools. We do not intend to comment on the differences, for example, that exist between caseworkers and psychotherapists with respect to length of treatment, type of patient, use of free association, adjustment to life-situation, or degree of personality reconstruction. It is not essential for us to distinguish between the psychoanalyst who diagnoses emotional difficulties in terms of intrapsychic conflicts and the psychoanalyst who places more emphasis on difficulties in communication and problems in interpersonal relations. We observe, but do not elaborate on the fact, that psychologists influenced by Carl R. Rogers are less concerned than other counselors or therapists with diagnosis and classification. What primarily concerns us are the uses of empathy, not the domain or the status of particular professional guilds. In this survey we are independent of in-group loyalties.

In a cross-disciplinary study such as this, it is hard to avoid a certain ambiguity in terms and frames of reference. The term "patient" is usually taken to refer to the person who seeks help from a psychiatrist or a psychoanalyst. The caseworker occasionally uses the term "patient" but more often makes reference to the "client." The term "counselee" occurs in the literature on counseling and personnel guidance. The chaplain or pastoral counselor uses no standard or professional nomenclature. It would be cumbersome to adhere to preferred usages in every case, although such consistency might please some specialists who are concerned with the domain and status of their particular discipline. For the most part we shall use the term "client" to refer to the individual seeking psychological help. Resource persons of a number of different disciplines and specialties will be referred to as counselors, therapists, interviewers, professionals, practitioners, or "empathizers."

The two main categories we shall use in grouping the professional roles in therapy with respect to the use of the empathic variable are "Insight" and "Relationship." These categories are far from satisfactory not only because they tend to overlap but because even those who are classified under "insight" also use a form of relationship, technically called "transference." One way of distinguishing between the two forms is to note that relationship in the second case is active and direct. In the first—the transference type—the relationship between the therapist and the client is less social or personal; the attitudes and feelings of the client toward the therapist consist in large part of a series of projections. The therapist himself remains relatively neutral and stays consistently within his disciplined and carefully circumscribed role. The only reason for using such admittedly doubtful categories is the fact they are fairly standard in the sources we have used. The professional who stresses insight and the establishment of "transference" is, of course, the Freudian analyst. Among those professionals who stress relationship therapy are psychiatrists, psychologists, caseworkers, counselors, clergymen, and educators. The psychiatric caseworker could actually be described in terms of a middle category including both insight and relationship. The same could be said for the psychoanalytically oriented psychiatrist. Psychoanalysts of the neo-Freudian schools could also be characterized as practitioners of insight and relationship therapy. It is likely that all forms of psychoanalysis include some element of relationship therapy, but in the classic Freudian model a personal *meeting* or *encounter* is discouraged.

The following chart may clarify the more explicit comparison that we shall make of the use and relevance of empathy in the two main types of therapy. We have noted the similarities and differences between the insight group, *I*, and the relationship group, *R*, using *I* to refer to roles which stress *insight* and a minimum of active or direct participation by the therapist, and *R* to designate the roles or points of view in therapy which stress the therapeutic value of more direct and active *relationship* by the therapist as well as emphasis in varying degrees on the value of insight.

Insight Therapy

Those who stress insight use empathy primarily as a means of gaining elusive knowledge of the inner experience and the unconscious processes of the client. For them empathy involves making a trial identification and calls for an internal, imaginative activity necessary in interpreting the dynamics of the client. Although they participate in the client's experience, all that they intend to share with the client is the results of this empathic activity of their own. They keep to a minimum the amount of emotional sharing that might be expected in a social encounter.

Freud recommended "abstinence" as the emotional climate best suited for analytic therapy (1955a, p. 162). He feared that affection or reassurance would diminish the amount of anxiety which would motivate the client to work through his fundamental problems. Comfort or relief might even discourage the client from remaining in therapy. An involvement of positive feeling by the therapist might impel the client to make a flight into health that would only be temporary. It might also induce the client to simulate a kind of recovery which was intended to please the therapist but which did not represent basic change or

The Place of Empathy in the *I* and *R* Types of Therapy

Therapist's Empathic Activity	Similarities between *I* and *R*	Differences between *I* and *R*
Purposes	To gain psychological understanding.	*I* more concerned with probing the unconscious.
	To assess intensity of client's feelings.	*R* more active in expressing empathic acceptance of client.
	To time the giving of interpretations.	*R* would permit client to identify with therapist as real person.
Quality of Relationship	Both would set limits and exercise controls.	*I* conceals his reactions and thus invites the emergence of projections or transference reactions by the client.
		R would participate more spontaneously and alternate between professional and personal levels of interaction.
Range and Depth of Participation	Both could identify intensely.	*I* more concerned with early stages of client's personality development.
		R more likely identifies with roles of client in recent past and present.
Expression of Affect		*I* more consistently anonymous and detached.
		R reveals more of self.

growth in the client himself. The client had to work out his own salvation, so to speak, and take responsibility for his own destiny as an independent and autonomous personality. What giving there was by the therapist was controlled and rational and consisted of communicating a bit of truth or a scientific observation achieved by the therapist through his own empathic and introspective activity. When he communicated, infrequently as that was, he detached himself from his empathic involvement and reported the insight he had gained. He would likely use empathy in order to ascertain the emotional readiness of his client to receive and assimilate his psychological interpretations. The therapist's empathy was a diagnostic tool or a barometer of feeling in the client rather than a sharing of emotional tone or a communication of feelings that may have been common to therapist and to client. The participation he expressed was primarily conscious and rational.

Empathic sharing is less important in insight therapy because what is believed to cure the patient is the insight into himself which he gains with the assistance of an expert consultant. If the client can grasp the meaning of the conflicts which impede him and if he can incorporate the data which have been uncovered in the course of his conferences with the therapist, he is capable of curing himself. The therapy is almost automatic. Once insight has been attained, the individual can be counted on to cure himself. Such self-understanding could not be attained without the assistance of a therapist who was skilled in making trial identifications, but it was not dependent upon a social and realistic relationship with the therapist as a specific and familiar individual.

When the client gains insight into himself, he is able to modify his patterns of thinking and feeling. He becomes free to use his emotional energies in new directions. He is no longer blocked. He is now capable of dealing with his impulses and his environment in a realistic and appropriate way. It is the awareness and the release of his own rational powers that turns the corner in his recovery. Insight leads to a readjustment of inner forces and a liberating of emotional energies. Because the client's conflicts were hidden and repressed, they were inaccessible and beyond his power to control. Once known, they become manageable. Energies previously bound up are now free for use and the client may be said to be cured.

The therapist himself could not have grasped the meaning of inner experiences which the client had repressed without the use of nonrational cognitive techniques. In his overt relationships with the client he remains relatively passive or neutral, a friendly but detached observer. He does not express his participation in the feelings of the client. To reveal his own feelings would be to distract the patient from the task of gaining insight into himself and his repressions. The therapist tries to conceal his own identity and personal characteristics. He inhibits his own responses in order to remain as anonymous as possible. He wishes to continue as the figure on whom the client may freely project feelings. After the psychological material is produced, the therapist introduces the interpretation which the client eventually understands and assimilates. Even the interpretation is detached from the personality of the therapist. It stands in its own right as a psychological fact. Personal and therefore inappropriate responses by the therapist are called "countertransference" and will be discussed further in Chapter V.

Even those who stress insight acknowledge that the therapeutic relationship is emotionally charged. In fact, the insight which is so important and critical for the client cannot be assimilated or worked through unless there is an investment of feeling. Freud recognized that the client required "a powerful, propelling force" to lead him toward insight and recovery. This force or positive feeling—which was called "transference"—"clothes the physician with authority and transforms itself into faith in his findings and his views" (1943, p. 387). Freud believed that faith and love were essential in the attitude of the client to his therapist. Such positive emotions spontaneously develop in the client and are not elicited by direct suggestions of the therapist or by repeated expressions of personal involvement on his part. They originate in the client and are projected upon the therapist. As the client achieves emotional independence, he no longer requires the force of this positive feeling for the therapist. The feelings that he projected upon the therapist and which were essential raw materials for therapy gradually fade away. In successful therapy, the temporary relationship dissolves. The client now enters into realistic social relationships outside the more artificial setting of therapy and invests his genuine and spontaneous feelings in everyday, nontherapeutic meetings.

The client, however, enters actively into a relationship or a series of relationships with the therapist. He casts the therapist in a number of roles, often transferring to him a number of responses and attitudes that originated in other situations. These feelings are called "transference feelings" and emerge in the therapeutic relationship because of the therapist's symbolic role as an authority or a healer. The therapist allows them to develop but he does little in a direct way to elicit or evoke them. He provides the client with a minimum of stimuli. His emotional neutrality or his lack of overt participation in the social relationship helps these feelings to emerge, but he attempts to restrict his direction or control over the associations of the client. He may be empathizing with the feelings of the client and attempting to penetrate the meaning of the associations and imaginative productions of the client, but seen from the point of view of the client, he is relatively inactive and reveals few cues concerning his own emotional states. The image the therapist presents is that of a friendly observer who participates but infrequently in the social interaction. When he does participate, his reactions are controlled and deliberate. The therapist does believe, however, in the value of an emotional experience as part of the client's learning experience. "The truth comes best in little pieces, slowly but surely, and with the emotions fully engaged in the acquisition" (Foulkes and Anthony, 1957, p. 201). If he manipulates his own response, it is for the purpose of permitting the client to have a *corrective emotional experience.* If he does not actively support the client in any more than a symbolic way, he also refrains from judging or disapproving of the client's responses. He is interested in them, accepts them, and wishes to understand them. He hopes that ultimately the client will be able to appreciate the feelings he experiences in the interview. If the client learns something from this therapeutic meeting and is able to modify his attitudes as a result of such insight, he will be free and resourceful in making his adjustments to the actual or real-life situations outside the interview. It is important, therefore, for the client to participate and to express his feelings and emotionally charged attitudes in the presence of the therapist.

Unless the client expresses such feelings, he is likely to miss being helped. One reason for this is that he will not provide the therapist with clues to his repressed or inaccessible conflicts. The therapist would be unable to identify because he would not receive enough emotional responses to stimulate his own empathic response. In the second place, if the client fails to express his feelings he does not become open to new learning. If he engages only a part of his own personality (i. e., his rational or intellectual side), he holds onto his customary patterns of feeling. If he does receive interpretations from his therapist, he may understand them intellectually but fail to incorporate them on other levels of his being. For intellectual appreciation to become insight and to gain the force capable of effecting personality changes it must be charged with feeling. It is important to repeat that in all of this emotional re-experiencing and active participation by the client, the therapist himself continues to remain relatively passive. He does not express his empathic understanding in a spontaneous way. He cultivates his self-experience as he identifies with the client, but he does not betray his internal activity. He thinks of himself as a catalyst for insight more than he does as a helping person whose own personal responses are relevant to successful therapy.

Therapists who stress insight more than personal relationship might agree that the problems of the client reflect some form of empathic deficiency dating from the client's childhood. He has not learned how to love. What he requires for his health is the recovery or the development of the ability to love. With this statement therapists ranging from Freud to Fromm would agree. The issue that divides therapists concerns the therapeutic techniques which are best suited to help the client master his deficiency. Those who favor insight therapy inhibit their own expression of empathy but invite the client to participate affectively in the interview. What is important is the insight the client gains, the freedom he will enjoy to empathize and establish relationships in realistic situations.

Critique of Relationship Therapy

The model of insight therapy which we just outlined is rarely followed by psychoanalysts and therapists with absolute fidelity. They modify their approach quite often in terms of particular clients, so that the line between insight and relationship therapy is not so sharp in practice as in theory. What is most pertinent to us as students of empathy is the fact that in relationship therapy, the doctor, the psychologist, or the counselor participates more actively. When the therapist does not attempt to screen his own identity so carefully and when he is concerned with personal as well as with transference relationships, he is likely to use his own empathies for more than diagnosis, evaluation, or interpretation. It is not necessarily true that such therapists follow more superficial treatment goals simply because they do not stress so strongly the uncovering of the unconscious material. In some therapeutic roles, to be sure, as in the case of brief supportive counseling or in guidance work, there is a greater concern with adjustment to specific life situations or with the removal of symptoms. But active relationship therapy can also be found in treatment situations where the goals are profound and far-reaching and where the therapist aims to help the client achieve basic personality or character changes.

What distinguishes the two forms of therapy, if at all, is a different theory about the therapist's activity as a change-agent. Empathy in the case of the insight therapist is more a tool for research. The discoveries he makes are offered to the client in the forms of facts or truths that are capable of liberating him from his conflicts and restoring him to fuller contact with reality. Empathy here is a means to an end. In the case of relationship therapy, empathy is recognized not only as a means of cognition but as a therapeutic force in itself. What liberates and cures is not only the insight of the therapist but also the energy of his own personality and his actual empathic engagement with the client. He is a catalyst of change not only because of skills in cognition but also because of empathic capacity for establishing therapeutic meetings or encounters with his client. Who and what he is are therefore more important as variables in effective therapy.

Ultimately the goal of relationship therapy, like that of insight therapy, is the restoration of the client's ability to use his own resources so that he can be more independent and resourceful, and freer in making decisions. Insight therapists may be more ambitious in that they may aspire to help the client realize new potentialities beyond the level of achievement attained by the client before requiring psychological aid. But both general forms of therapy have as their goal the liberation of the client's own energies so that he becomes more capable of independent and realistic action.

We must look at the question of technique also. Does the therapist enter into a relationship in a more controlled and detached way, exploiting the symbolic aspects of his role and maintaining a fairly anonymous identity or does he actively participate in a two-way relationship, investing more of his own emotional responses and sharing them with his client? Those who are impressed with the effectiveness of relationship therapy believe that the client achieves or recovers his independent capacities because he experiences growth in the relationship he has with a therapist who empathizes more openly. Those who are closely identified with insight therapy raise technical objections to this claim, asserting that the establishment and clarification of transference relationships is the *sine qua non* of their goal of uncovering what is repressed and of making it accessible to rational examination and control.

Even insight therapists recognize that relationship therapy is appropriate in the treatment of children. They feel free to empathize directly with younger patients and to offer encouragement and acceptance more openly. When dependent needs are great, they will depart from the classic model of detachment. They will make the same adjustment when dealing with adult patients who do not have sufficient ego strength to tolerate the emotional deprivation involved in the more purely analytical therapy. Without yielding his basic conviction regarding insight as the most desirable form of therapy, Freud indicated that the future would likely bring many changes and that one of these would be greater activity on the part of the therapist. What Freud refers to as "suggestion" in the following statement, we would equate with more active empathy or a communication of feeling or concern by the therapist to the client. "It is very probable, too, that the large scale application of our therapy will compel us to alloy the pure gold of analysis freely with the copper of suggestion" (1955a, pp. 167-168).

At least a few of Freud's followers believe that the pure gold of analysis or insight has not always proved to be as effective or as relevant as Freud thought. Franz Alexander has observed that some patients in psychoanalysis achieve profound personality change without attaining the self-knowledge or appreciation of the emotional forces in their development which accounted for the genesis of their neurotic problems (1960, pp. 119-120). He noted too that others who have undergone insight therapy have not experienced personality change even though they have gained a profound awareness of factors in their life history of which they had little consciousness. He seems to suggest that the interpersonal factor in treatment is likely to be emphasized in future developments of psychoanalytic technique. This kind of thinking is of course quite central in the neo-Freudian therapies associated with the names of Harry Stack Sullivan and Frieda Fromm-Reichmann. It is likely that in the future the distinctions between insight and relationship therapy will be less significant and that empathy will therefore find a wider use among practitioners of intensive psychotherapy or psychoanalysis.

Another reason why empathy as personal relationship may be increasingly emphasized has to do with the changing character of our society and the kinds of problems for which clients seek therapy. Many therapists feel that active relationship by the therapist is essential in treating individuals who live in an alienated society, who experience crises in identity, and who suffer from the anxiety of living in a normless society. It is likely that an increasing number of clients will come for help with character disorders and that they will be suffering from diffuse anxiety. Allen Wheelis has observed that classic analysis was quite successful with individuals who lived in a more stable and moralistic society and suffered from specific illnesses which could be diagnosed with relative ease. Insight is less successful when the client's character is warped and his personality is not well integrated. "The conflict is less likely to manifest itself in the form of specific symptoms or to have the quality of a syndrome, but is vague and amorphous, pervading the entire personality" (1958, pp. 41-42).

Some of the revisions of classic Freudian therapy can therefore be seen as something more than heresy to the tradition of insight therapy and may very well represent modifications which are made necessary by a new group of clients whose emotional problems are more interpersonal. Such problems may be more amenable to forms of therapy where empathy is used for establishing relationships as well as for purposes of cognition. In a more other-directed society where skills in communication are more essential for adjustment and where values are determined by an ever changing present rather than by a rigid and established tradition, it is likely that new emphases in therapy will occur. One psychoanalyst has observed,

the patient of today suffers most under the problem of what he should believe in and who he should—or, indeed, might—become; while the patient of early psychoanalysis suffered most under inhibitions which prevented him from being what and who he thought he knew he was (Erikson, 1950, p. 239).

In such a society with its problems of character and of identity and with its preoccupation with morale rather than morals, the therapist meets new types of clients. Their expectations are different as are their needs. Therapy may likely use more of the "copper of suggestion" without sharing Freud's opinion, still held in more orthodox Freudian circles, that more active therapy is only a dilution of "genuine" therapy.

Features of Relationship Therapy

What are some of the specific features of relationship therapy? It is necessary to define more clearly the role of acceptance and participation. The practitioners of more active empathy communicate certain attitudes to the client which the insight therapist would acknowledge only indirectly and rarely share with the client except by implication. Even when they attach greater importance to their role as mentors of psychological truth and rational insight, some insight therapists refer to an almost personal involvement with the client. Karl Menninger, for example, stresses "the soft but persistent voice of the intellect" among the factors which turn the corner in therapy but adds another factor consisting of the constructive effect of the personality of the therapist himself. The client is measurably helped by ". . . the example of the psychoanalyst himself—his poise, his patience, his fairness, his consistency, his rationality, his kindliness, in short —his *real* love for the patient" (1958, p. 157).

What is acknowledged as a minor theme in therapy by Menninger, a representative of the mainstream of the Freudian tradition in psychoanalysis, is unhesitatingly espoused in relationship therapy. The therapist's own personality and his actual feelings for the client are active ingredients in the cure. In answering the fundamental question raised by Menninger himself —"what stabilizes the patient?"—practitioners of relationship therapy point to the acceptance which the patient experiences in the presence of his therapist and the identification he makes with the newer and more constructive image his therapist has of him. Something changes within the client as a result of his intimate association with the helping agent. He participates in a new group which was formed because of the reciprocal empathy between his therapist and himself. In this new group, which might be called a miniature community, to use Norman Cameron's phrase, the individual gains support, senses a cohesive strength, and gains not only intellectual but emotional feedback from his fellow participant. This experience of intimacy and of full communication will of course be relatively brief, lasting only as long as the professional therapeutic relationship continues. To some extent it is artificial and unconventional. Yet at the same time, it is an actual meeting between two persons in which the partner seeking help finds new dimensions to his own personality and gains a new sense of freedom to draw on his own intellectual and emotional capacities.

So often the patient enters therapy because of a lack of empathy with himself as well as with others. The recognition of his complete acceptance by the other member of the group becomes for him a releaser-mechanism, freeing his energies for creative uses.

Carl R. Rogers' description of the therapist as a companion is very much to the point:

> the relationship which I have found helpful is characterized by a sort of transparency on my part, in which my real feelings are evident; by an acceptance of this other person as a separate person with value in his own right, and by a deep empathic understanding which enables me to see his private world through his eyes. When these conditions are achieved, I become a companion to my client, accompanying him in the frightening search for himself, which he now feels free to undertake (1954, p. 4).

Acceptance by another person is not enough in itself. According to Rollo May, this is the error implicit in certain forms of "relationship therapy." The therapeutic advantage of such acceptance lies in the fact that the client is now released to experience himself more fully and thus to progress in realizing his own potentialities. "The acceptance by another person, such as the therapist, shows the patient that he no longer needs to fight his main battle on the front of whether anyone else, or the world can accept him; the acceptance *frees* him to experience his own being" (1958, p. 45). It can be seen that the ability to "experience his own being" means a recovery of the patient's ability to empathize with himself. Self-awareness based on internal dialogue or communication is a goal common to both insight and relationship therapy. The relative power of insight or of an experience of mutuality in evoking such self- or auto-empathy is the subject of the controversy.

Acceptance relieves the client of the burden of using self-defeating defense mechanisms which have blocked his ability to gain objective knowledge of himself and of others and which have distorted his role-taking. The fear of being unacceptable and the sense of isolation evoked by his lack of communication with others has made him insecure and anxious. He misses the gratifications of being in touch with himself and with others. He overcomes his failure in empathy when he comes to experience the sensitive and genuine empathy of his therapist. He is able to sense the therapist's identification with him and with neglected and isolated facets of his own personality. He feels that his therapist does not look upon him as an example of certain categories of emotional illness which can be diagnosed psychologically and interpreted in standardized frames of reference. While the client stands to gain by absorbing the scientific and valid information that the therapist is capable of offering him, he is likely to profit as much or more by the activity of relating to the therapist and of feeling that the therapist, in turn, is involved or connected with him. He experiences the therapist's interest in him, his concern for his welfare, and his confidence in his own powers. There is a healthy contagion of the therapist's confidence and rational faith in him. At the same time he assimilates some of the qualities of the therapist himself and grows through this identification with the therapist as a fellow human who has achieved psychological security. It is not likely, as we shall indicate in the next chapter, that he could make this essential identification with the therapist if he did not vividly experience the therapist's active concern with him and lively respect for his inner strength and latent powers.

The therapist attempts to give the client the feeling of being accepted. He tries to be more than a symbol of the healing profession and enters into the world of the client who thus benefits by a new kind of experience. Adrian L. van Kaam's description of this experience is useful:

The experience of "really feeling understood" is a perceptual-emotional Gestalt: A subject, perceiving that a person coexperiences what things mean to the subject and accepts him, feels, initially, relief from experiential loneliness, and, gradually, safe experiential communion with that person and with that which the subject perceives this person to represent (1959, p. 69).

The terms "coexperience" and "communion" can be taken as synonyms for empathy or identification. The value for the client of such empathy on the part of the therapist amounts, of course, to more than relief. It is a constructive, re-educating, and therapeutic experience in itself.

Activity is initiated by the therapist as well as by the client. In insight therapy, where the therapist remains neutral and fairly anonymous, the client often projects different roles upon the therapist. In the transference, he may respond to the therapist in many different ways. He structures the situation in his own imagination because of his own needs and his associations. The very neutrality of the therapist permits and almost invites the client to cast him in different roles. He may be father, brother, or mother, depending upon the associations of the client and the kinds of problems he is working through. The therapist allows these projections to take place and at certain intervals explains to the client the meaning of these associations. There he is a quiet teacher interpreting symbolic meanings and emotional responses. Essentially it is the client who is the playwright in the dramas. The emotions engaged in such imaginary dramas are primarily the client's. The therapist may make trial identifications with the patient, but this role-taking is covert and is done only for the purpose of increasing his appreciation of the client's feelings. The therapist acts only on the basis of his professional role and when he speaks he rarely departs from a consistent and carefully defined pattern.

The situation is different in relationship therapy where the therapist, far less anonymous or neutral, genuinely participates in the dialogue. He may allow himself to respond to the client as if he were in the role of the client's father or brother. He may enact the role of the client as the child or adolescent he may have been. At the same time, he may also respond to the client as a friend and contemporary. He departs from the fixed professional or standardized role and shares with his client some of his actual and spontaneous personal responses. He becomes a fellow group member and participates in the emotional interchange. Such meetings or encounters with the client are not heart-to-heart talks between individuals engaged in mutual aid. The therapist is presumably stronger and more resourceful. He is a friend in some ways, but he is also more than a friend because of his own training in therapy, his insight into himself, and his professional commitment to help the client. He still maintains his professional concern and self-discipline, even if his participation is not as structured as would be the case in insight therapy. He takes a wide repertory of roles in terms of the needs of the client and the changing requirements of empathy, but he does not abandon his professional identity.

The social or interpersonal character of this form of therapy sets it apart from the more classic insight therapy where the therapist remains essentially detached from his client. In relationship therapy, it is the communication and the coexperiencing which cures. Both client and therapist share in a relationship. Both are present and both are real. Growth of self takes place in actively empathic relationships, to paraphrase Martin Buber:

For the inmost growth of the self is not accomplished, as people like to suppose today, in man's relation to himself, but in the relations between the one and the other, between men, that is, preeminently in the mutuality of the making present—in the making present of another self and in the knowledge that one is made present in his own self by the other—together with the mutuality of acceptance, affirmation, and confirmation (1953, p. 104).

The possibilities for error and failure can obviously be great in the form of therapy being sketched here. For this form of therapy to be successful the client must enter into a dependent relationship with the therapist, who in turn must be prepared to control and to vary the degree of his involvement with the client. The therapist obviously runs greater risks of involvement in this situation than in insight therapy where his activity is minimal and he maintains a consistent and familiar role.

From this chapter which has dealt with the contributions of empathy to the recovery of the client and to the skill of the therapist, we now turn to an analysis of the practice of empathy as a technical and human skill on the part of the therapist. In Chapter V, we examine the qualifications and prerequisites for effective empathy, considering the functions of empathy as a means of cognition and as a therapeutic attitude. In Chapter VI, we review some of the common as well as less common errors and failures in empathizing.

V

THE EFFECTIVE EMPATHIZER

WHAT ARE the prerequisites for the skillful and effective use of empathy by the therapist? In earlier chapters we examined the basic process of empathy. What now concerns us are the conditions most conducive to creative empathy. Even though we now deal with the *how* of empathy, we have no intention of prescribing a technique. What is essential is an awareness of the ways the effective empathizer uses himself and an appreciation of the personal characteristics that correlate well with empathy as a technique of cognition and as a healing relationship. What factors lead to the most direct and complete participation in the inner experience of another person and to the achievement of the greatest possible similarity or identity with the client?

We have already discussed the pertinence of innate and constitutional factors so that we need only to recall that some of the conditions of empathic sensitivity are simply given. Those therapists who are born healers have an easy and natural appreciation for nuances of feelings in others. Their built-in sensitivities and rich imaginative powers account for their knack for communicating nonverbally and for apprehending cues that others inevitably miss. For other therapists with less natural affinity for empathic penetration, the question of enhancing and developing subjective processes becomes more relevant. There is probably a point beyond which they cannot go even with the most extensive training and experience.

Gifted empathizers are exceptional, and effective empathizers are by no means common. In addition to what advantages they may have in terms of natural empathic sensitivity, professionals must be capable of disengaging themselves from their identifications with others and of taking an outside view of their own subjective processes. This is essential if they are to check their empathic impressions against their clinical knowledge and their observations. They are successful in empathizing when they balance empathic involvement with rational judgment and when they avoid either extreme of under- or overidentifying.

Difficult as it is to discuss the ideal conditions for empathy without commenting simultaneously on the errors and failures, we shall specify the correlates of empathy and defer to the following chapter, with some risk of repetition, an outline of the more common mistakes in empathy. The chart below provides an overview of factors that correlate positively and negatively with the richest use of the inner processes we are describing.

The qualities of the good empathizer in human relations are similar in many respects to the qualities of the gifted artist. There is the same need to involve the emotions, to relax conscious controls, and to permit oneself to be projected into other objects. In Barbara Low's words,

The essential process appears to be a form of introjection and projection directed toward the material presented by the patient, a situation which parallels the relationship between the artist and the external world upon which he works (1935, p. 3).

The therapist works under unusually stressful conditions because the materials presented by his client are constantly changing and because he cannot stop the motion of his own imagery and cap-

Empathic Processes in the Therapist

The Potential or Ideal (Chapter V)	Misuse or Distortion in Practice (Chapter VI)
Participates in experience of client by identifying or merging.	Remains emotionally absent or projects. Under- or overidentifies.
Experiences real love and care for the client.	Experiences "therapeutic furor." Has negative or positive countertransference.
Accepts himself.	Has negative attitude toward self and experiences client in same way.
Experiences motility and alternation of feeling-states. Spontaneity.	Cannot stabilize his moods. Repertory of feeling-states is limited. Unable to let go.
Tolerates anxiety.	Preoccupied with defenses or security operations.
Participates deeply and over full range of client's feeling-states, roles, life situations.	Concerned only with the unconscious. Neglects client's world and goals.
Has courage and patience to suspend judgment.	Relies on feeling-states only. Categorizes too quickly.

ture it in words like a poet or in forms like an artist. The artistic medium he uses is himself, and no matter how innately talented or rigorously trained, he can never be sure that his psyche is properly attuned. His own feelings are volatile and he cannot exercise the same control over them that the artist can over sounds, colors, or designs. Obviously it is much more difficult to identify the successes of the therapist than those of the artist. One criterion would be the consensus of the client. Another would be the changes in the behavior of the client which we presume were evoked at least in part by his empathic relationship with his therapist.

Flexibility of Ego Boundaries

Like the creative artist who feels himself into his material, the effective empathizer is capable of blending himself with his subject. There are any number of familiar synonyms which express this process of involvement on levels other than the rational, the verbal, and the deliberate:

	is transported	is immersed in
	becomes full of	shares or participates in
The	is pervaded by	responds to
empathizer	is attuned to	merges with
	abandons himself in	forgets himself in
	is caught up with	is absorbed by

Using a more technical frame of reference, we could say that the good empathizer has flexible ego boundaries. He has the ideal ego formation which Paul Federn has described: "An ego formation in which the ego boundaries can change rapidly and easily but remain stable at any time if a standpoint must be held or defended, should be considered ideal" (1952, p. 344). He is capable of moving with ease from one state of feeling or "state of mind" (ego state) to another. This means that he does not draw exclusively on his conscious or secondary processes in his interactions with others. He is more versatile than the ordinary adult who has disciplined himself to suppress his playful instincts and to cultivate his critical intelligence. He is capable of detaching himself from objects in his environment, of suspending emotional involvements, of analyzing people and phenomena in terms of rational principles. The good empathizer must be exceptionally well trained in objective analysis, but what is more distinctive in his case is his inner freedom on occasion to abandon this rational, mature ego. He is capable of taking many roles easily and can move from one ego state to another without conflict or without self-consciousness. When he surrenders himself to other processes and to other levels of feeling, he experiences wider frontiers of awareness that would otherwise have been limited by the range of his conscious intelligence and memory. He reduces the social distance between the client and himself by relaxing the boundaries of an ego which commonly resists invasion by other ego states.

The ego boundaries are relaxed in two directions: first, vis-à-vis the client and second, vis-à-vis different facets and strata of personality within the therapist himself. Instead of isolating the client in a prescribed field of observation, the therapist moves into the experience of the client by projecting himself into the client or identifying with him and by taking the client's experience into himself or, more symbolically, by incorporating or introjecting the client. Through these processes, his own ego boundaries are extended to include the client. With respect to himself, the therapist relaxes his own controls and becomes capable of communicating with one or more of the many ego states that form part of his own person and which in ordinary communication he would exclude from his consciousness or at least avoid cultivating, even if they were to intrude.

We can therefore speak of the therapist as relaxing the ego boundaries between his adult ego and states of feeling still surviving from earlier levels of his own development. In his communication with the client, he may respond with the simplicity and directness of the child, or with some of his own anxieties as an adolescent. His own experiences are invested in the contact with the client, so that when he responds, more of himself is engaged than just his conscious awareness of himself as a professional. He draws on a whole repertory of feelings and responses because he moves easily from one level of fantasy and experience to another. He does not feel that sensations and responses which appear unaccountably and erratically must be suppressed. He does not inhibit his own spontaneity and compel himself to concentrate on a rational understanding of what his client may be saying. He enters into the experience and, if he is creative in his empathy, he may respond on different levels in ways that are unpredictable and uncontrollable. The freer his ego boundaries the richer will be his experience of the other person and the richer will be his own associations to this experience. He is able to take in more of the client's experience and to experience it more intensely. He has not only the one radar—his perceiving and reflective ego— but also a whole series of radars, located at strategic points and capable of receiving impressions from many directions and at different levels.

We should not infer that the good empathizer attunes his radar or series of radars at will. There is a kind of empathic identification by which he may consciously try to put himself into the role of the other person. He might attempt to conjure up the situation in which his client finds himself and set about to experience within himself a series of responses to the images set up in his mind by this series of controlled associations. He puts together some of the cues which the client expresses to him. Such empathy calls for the interviewer to be a playwright, designing a scene in which he will insert himself as an actor.

But such *conscious empathizing* means that the empathizer holds back from a fuller participation. As an artist, he knows in advance much of the design that he wishes to create and imposes it upon his subject. He remains at a distance from the subject, and within himself he remains fairly consistently on one ego level.

Identification or empathy in depth is not a conscious or deliberate process. Almost by definition it refers to an unconscious projection of oneself and the introjection of another. Our earlier discussion referred to the primitive and instinctual origins of such processes. The good empathizer is one who is capable of drawing on more primitive and prelogical levels of his own being, so that his experience of others is probably far more direct and intensive. If this is so, then it is not likely that he could conjure such feelings at will or deliberately recall them as needed. The very consciousness of the intent would inhibit the spontaneity of the process.

Although we speak of empathy as taking place on different levels, it is probably true that every case of genuine identification includes an element of the unconscious and a relaxation of rational controls. The good empathizer is able to surrender himself to such unconscious or preconscious activity. When he detaches himself from his client, he is fully capable of using his rational powers for purposes of analysis and interpretation. At the moment of genuine empathic activity *in situ*, there is no question but that momentarily he loses awareness of self and freely moves into the field of another person. He must be able to interrupt this process by an act of will, but in the moments of empathic projection, he is free-floating, susceptible to the waves of his own unconscious and his relatively uncontrolled responses to the client's feelings. Since empathy is involuntary, the therapist does not even attempt to direct his responses. He is open to suggestion, as it were, excitable by the stimulus of the client, to his words, his gestures, to his person. The therapist cannot lower his threshold of attention by an act of will or of conscious ego. Paradoxically, even such an attempt to change himself would increase his self-consciousness and defeat his purpose.

We shall note a number of personal characteristics, like acceptance of self and toleration of anxiety, which correlate positively with flexibility of ego boundaries. The therapist interested in expanding his ego boundaries could at most cultivate self-knowledge and try to open himself to the feelings of others. He might gain a certain proficiency in role-taking by participating in psychodrama. Such cultivation of self can be no more than a preliminary exercise. In the actual encounter with another person, the therapist does little more than exclude other interests. He becomes purposeless and passive. The client's words and feelings act directly upon him so that his own responses cannot be calculated. Contact between the client and the good therapist is all the more immediate because the therapist's conscious ego does not filter or channel the message. He is present but his presence is not the usual ego state of the receiver who tries to codify incoming data. Nor is it a single ego state, motionless like a radar frozen on its axis which only picks up signals emanating from one direction. Just as the radar must be free to rotate, so the therapist must be mobile and sensitive, capable of shifting from one self or ego state to another. One does not "make a trial identification," because *making* implies directed activity. An identification takes place; it happens to us. The most that we can do is "to let go." We do not pretend, imitate, or project. We are acted upon. The good empathizer does not manipulate the client to stimulate him in a particular way, nor does he try to exercise control over the easy and automatic ways he responds, resonates, or reverberates to the stimulus. He interferes neither with the client nor with himself.

Obviously the therapist will ask brief questions in the interview. Such questions may be empathic in tone and intent, but they have their source in reason and detachment. Because they represent the conscious will of the interviewer they could not be described as empathic participation.

This discussion rests on the assumption that every individual possesses a number of ego states or levels of conciousness. Freud spoke of a number of states of consciousness which may be unknown to us and unknown to each other. The good therapist would have an exceptionally labile constitution which permits him to move rapidly from one ego state to another. He succeeds in opening up contact between the several ego states of his client and himself. Freud's advice to therapists is well known:

Experience soon showed that the attitude which the analytical physician could most advantageously adopt was to surrender himself to his own unconscious mental activity, in a state of easy and impartial attention, to avoid as far as possible reflection and the construction of conscious expectations, not to try and fix anything that he heard particularly in his memory, and by these means to catch the drift of the patient's unconscious with his own unconscious (1955c, p. 239).

Of particular importance is Freud's use of the term "surrender." What the therapist gives up is the disciplined conscious attention stipulated in conventional research. Others, influenced by Freud, have spoken of the regression of the therapist. Ernest Kris's concept of "regression in the service of the ego" explaining the creative activities of the artist has been used by Roy A. Schafer to account for slipping into more primitive and childlike techniques of response which are part of the operation of empathy (1959, pp. 130-131). The good empathizer is therefore one who can regress easily and permit himself to use more primary processes of communication so often set aside in the task of manipulating objects in a reasonable and rational way. Such regression reawakens responses and needs long forgotten by the therapist. They could not be recalled at will. They emerge through their own impetus as part of a freely flowing associative process.

When the good empathizer regresses, he does more than recollect or re-experience events out of his own childhood. He also engages in a playful kind of activity as he inwardly imitates the events in the life of his client that may be current as well as past. His activity is regressive only in the sense that it calls for a relaxed and unstructured experience which we associate with the fantasy of the child or the poetic license which we grant to the creative artist. He uses spontaneous and nonrational techniques of communicating. To say that he "regresses" is to indicate that he uses more primary processes; it does not mean that he is lapsing from a necessarily higher stage of personality development. The good empathizer is able to shift from role to role in his fantasy. His repertory of roles, as Roy Schafer observed, is wide and may include figures from the present as well as from the past. "In his empathic functioning the therapist is in certain respects mother, father, sibling, child, and lover of the patient as well as, through introjection, the patient himself" (1959, p. 354).

Participating in the roles of parent, sibling, and so on, the empathizer re-experiences the situation of the client as well as his own situation. He not only gains access to the meaning of these experiences in his unconscious but he also shares them in a more active way. It is a human participation and as such involves more than the intuitive, direct grasp of alien objects. More than the empathizer's unconscious gets drawn into the communication. He is not only an instrument for detection but a partner in the two way process of communication. When he succeeds—and we may speak here of empathic cognition and of empathic relationship—he is actively forming new and changing combinations, fusing with ego states in the client and with ego states in himself that may have been latent.

Because the empathizer is open to the experiences of others and because he is capable of taking those experiences into himself and feeling them as though they were his own, he not only penetrates the deeper layers of the other person but also becomes related to him. What he experiences should not be considered only as a vicarious experience or an *as-if* phenomenon. *As-if* is a logical term. Psychologically speaking, the empathizer is not conscious that the experience he imitates was actually felt originally by another person. Were he conscious of this, he could not abandon his own identity (i.e., the fixed role of intellectual observer). Moreover, when different ego states of his own are reactivated, he does not sense them as lapses or regressions from his normal conscious self. What he experiences is vivid and concrete, whether it is the internalized experience of another self or unsuspected and unfamiliar ego states within himself.

Even the best empathizer can only approximate the exact experience of others. But within the limits of human communication, he feels what the other feels and at the moment of such fantasy or experience there is no division between himself and another self. He becomes the client in the same way that the reader of a poem merges with its author. Henri Bergson's report of his own aesthetic experience is very much to the point:

When a poet reads me his verses, I can interest myself enough in him to enter into his thought, put myself into his feelings, live over again the simple state he has broken into phrases and words. I sympathize then with his inspiration, I follow it with a continuous movement which is, like the inspiration itself, an undivided act (1911a, p. 209).

The ego boundaries of the therapist expand to include ego states in others and in himself. Only when he has moved from empathy to objective scrutiny do such boundaries become stabilized once more. The therapist then resumes his conventional role as a professional and detached observer. Subsequently, he may abandon the interlude of self-awareness and conscious reflection and plunge into other empathic experiences. His formidable skill consists of alternating between empathic experiences and analysis of such experience. He can do this without danger to himself and with great advantage for his client if he possesses flexible ego boundaries. To this must be added the component, soon to be discussed, of a secure ego of his own.

Respect for the Integrity of the Client

A second feature of effective empathy is the ability to distinguish between oneself and the other person. No matter how

vividly the other person is experienced nor how intensely the
therapist participates in the qualities and nuances of feeling of
the other person, he is able to tighten the boundaries of his own
ego. He achieves a high degree of similarity, it is true, but whether
he is similar in reality or in imaginative empathy, the therapist
is disciplined to remind himself that after all he is communicating
with another person. He must therefore be capable of detaching
himself from his involvement in the feelings of the other person.
Much more will be said in Chapter VI of the harm done by
empathic overidentification, by sympathy, and by projection.
The mark of the good empathizer is the respect he has for the
integrity of his client. Even though at times he may extricate
himself with great difficulty from the experience of intense
empathy, he is capable of distinguishing what belongs to him
and what belongs to the other person. Here again the regard he
has for himself and the knowledge he has of his own impulses and
needs enable him to resist the continued pull which the other
person may exercise over him in an almost hypnotic way. It is
a delicately balanced ability which the empathizer has of being
able to plunge into the sea of experience of another person and
yet be able to climb out on the shore and regain his own sense of
self. Even when he dives in deeply (or is drawn in), he has a
lifeline tied around him. This image of immersion and extrica-
tion, which both Martin Buber and Theodor Reik contributed,
makes us appreciate the paradoxical talent of the empathizer. He
can abandon himself and yet regain himself through an act of
will.

The therapist often finds personal gratification in his empathic
communion with his client. Some of his own needs are undoubt-
edly met. His own emotions are stimulated. But if he is a
disciplined interviewer he is able to recognize the dangers of his
involvement. He recognizes that empathy may provide a narcissistic gratification and his very consciousness of this possibility
alerts him. What keeps him from gratifying his own needs at the
expense of the patient is his awareness that the purpose of his
empathic activity is help for the patient and not himself. He
feels free to invest himself in the empathic experience because
he knows that the risk he takes is part of a therapeutic program.

If he uses his subjective powers, he does this with full knowledge that his goal is *objective knowledge* of his client. The therapist recognizes that he must see the patient as he is, objectively and actually, rather than as he would like the patient to be. Even when he takes the role of healer or change agent, he is careful to help the client move in directions that are best for him. He avoids projecting private values, concentrating instead on evoking experiences of growth which reflect the nature of the client and his own needs. The therapist may take the role of teacher or mentor, but when and if he does, it is not to win converts to his own values. Even if we feel that the therapist may be far more active than the classical model of the Freudian analyst, we can still subscribe to Freud's caution that "the patient should be educated to liberate and fulfill his own nature, not to resemble ourselves" (1955a p. 165). The good empathizer tries to achieve a similarity with the client and thus to penetrate into the client's world but resists the temptation to make the client similar to himself or even to distort his perception of the client by seeing him only as a potential replica of himself.

The good counselor or therapist must be able to detach himself so that he may, in Barbara Low's poetic words, "reflect in tranquility" upon the emotions he has experienced in moments of empathic involvement. He is able to detach himself not only from the ego states and the roles of the client but also from the associations and feelings which were activated in himself by this communication. He is a participant observer even with respect to his own experiences. In Erik Erikson's words, "the mental healer must divide himself as well as the patient into an observer and an observed" (1957, p. 88). All of his sensations, his images, and his inner experiences call for objective analysis and for interpretation. The good empathizer is therefore able to achieve a psychic distance and from this more rational and conscious position reflect on the meaning of the experiences he undergoes. Saving him from error is his professional commitment to his role as a change agent. The stimulus for his inner experience originated with the client. It is true that some of his imaginative experience in moments of empathy consists of memories and associations of his own psychic and emotional life. But even these, however vividly experienced as belonging to him, become relevant to his role as therapist only in so far as they may conceivably be helpful to the client. Such insight as the therapist may get into himself in such moments is a by-product of his therapeutic role. He is careful to avoid confusing the truths he has learned about himself with what the client needs to know and what will be helpful to him. His specific purpose, wrote Rollo May, is to help "the other person to bring to birth something from within himself." He is only a midwife, because the creative act itself is the province of the other person (1958, p. 84). Creative experiences within the interviewer which mark his own growth are only incidental to therapeutic work. There the focus must be on the objective needs of the client.

The skillful empathizer can interrupt the empathic process and relieve its intensity. He has a rich talent for imaginative projection and enjoys ego boundaries that are permeable, but his need for vicariously experiencing the emotions of others is minimal. He can therefore pull himself out of the involvement, even though it almost possesses him while running its course. The effective empathizer has something of the emotional susceptibility to the moods of others which in exaggerated forms is found in the hysteric but is protected by a stable sense of his own identity and a recognition of the separate and objective existence of other selves.

Self-Knowledge and Self-Acceptance

The effective empathizer is capable of feeling himself into a variety of states within a particular client as well as responding empathically to a variety of different clients. He is distinguished also by the intensity of his participation. These two characteristics derive from his inner security. He possesses a strong ego and his empathies with himself include not only self-knowledge or cognition but also a positive or loving attitude toward himself. Unlike the more insecure individual who is able to identify only with those who already resemble him, he is able to feel himself at one with those who appear to be different from him. He does not require the empathic support which the other person might give him and he is willing to risk experiencing the unknown and the different. His empathies are deeper also because he can tolerate the anxieties of the other person which he vicariously experiences and because he is capable also of dealing with anxieties of his own that are reactivated by the stimulus coming from the other person. So much of his therapeutic success is a by-product of the kind of person he is.

The emphasis upon the personality of the therapist has been one of the most important contributions of psychoanalysis. Unfortunately, so much stress is laid on self-knowledge that the role of character is underestimated. In the skillful use of empathy, the interviewer requires not only the elimination of errors and blind spots in his own personality but also the more positive attributes of self-trust and self-acceptance. The effective empathizer is more than a nearly perfect cognitive instrument which has been ground and polished in the most meticulous self-study and in the training analysis which is now prerequisite for the psychoanalytic profession. He is capable also of trusting himself and his reactions, of experiencing himself in a positive and even joyous way. While his self-understanding should be as profound and as thorough as possible, he would be free from the temptation to use his self-cognition as a defense against his own spontaneity. While he is free from self-deception, he is not so painfully self-conscious that he always remains an observer of his own reactions. He is not preoccupied with maintaining rigid control over the course of his interview nor is he concerned with the possible threat of being caught off guard by unexpected developments in his relationship with his client. He is not defensive vis-à-vis the client, since he has no fixed, professional image that he must defend. He trusts his own impulses and accepts his own responses and, enjoying this inner security, he finds that he is open to absorb the experiences of others and to identify with them freely.

Self-knowledge is important, as we shall soon emphasize, but the model empathizer requires a spontaneous and self-respecting character whose emotional needs are stabilized. Such a person is fully capable of giving love and acceptance to others but does not either require or seek such acceptance from his clients. Such

needs as he may have to give love are themselves within reasonable
limits and do not interfere with his objectivity. Izette de Forest
has underscored the importance of the personality variable in
successful therapy:

Whatever the psychotherapist may accomplish with his patient, he
accomplishes because of *who and what he is*. His skill, his empathic
capacity, his originality of theory and practice, are the expressions
of his integrated, self-controlled, and ripened personality (1954, p.
188).

Perhaps only in the creative arts and in religious experience
is the quality of self-experience so important. If the therapist's
attitude toward himself is open and creative, he will be sensitive
to the possibilities of growth in his client. His own self-respect
keeps him from projecting unsolved problems of his own onto his
client and enables him to respond to the potential for self-respect
which still remains within the client even though the evidence
for this potential is unseen. Fromm observed that "the way one
experiences others is not different from the way one experiences
oneself" (1947, p. 73). Because the good empathizer experiences
himself as someone who is growing and alive, he is capable of
empathizing with the fuller humanity that can be realized by the
client himself. The character of the therapist does not have to be
all sweetness and serenity, since his own struggles, past and
present, sharpen his sensitivity to the ongoing problems of his
client. What distinguishes him from his client, among other things,
is the relative success he has in dealing with his own conflicts. He
still has available to himself the memory and the experience of
those conflicts, if not some still active and growing edges in his
own personality. His *self-experience* helps him to identify with
some of the client's present problems. There is nothing in the
client's experiences that is completely alien to the therapist himself. He has the same instinctual endowment and the same
potentialities. His self-knowledge and his self-recollection make
him sensitive to the present which the client experiences, while
his own greater personal integration and self-mastery enable him
to identify with some of the more creative and healthy potentialities within the client. In any case, it is the sensitivity to self that
is critical for his role as empathizer. In effective empathy, he may

use some of his own conflicts for understanding the client's impasse, yet his self-acceptance alerts him to the more creative side of his client's personality.

The practitioner is not free from anxiety. His own anxieties as well as those of his client are re-experienced. Because of his own fundamental self-acceptance, he can taste the anxiety of the other person without fear of being damaged. He is open to the contagion of the anxious feelings of his client because his own emotional energies are not bound up in defending himself. He is free to experiment with his own reactions because he knows which situations evoke his own anxiety and because he trusts his power to tolerate anxiety.

He appreciates the fact that it is actually necessary for him to share the anxieties of his client. For one thing, his own anxiety serves as a barometer for the level of anxiety in his client. He really has no instrument or machine which he can substitute in making such an assessment. From observing his own reactions to the patient, he gains an appreciation of the degree of anxiety his patient has and the situations which evoke anxiety in the patient. His own feelings of discomfort enable him to understand what his client experiences and how intense these experiences are. Frieda Fromm-Reichmann has described the function of the therapist's empathy as

an important divining rod for the discovery of many emotional experiences of patients which might otherwise remain undiscovered and hidden for a long time, as in the case of a psychiatrist who would not feel free to use his own anxiety as a guide to anxiety-provoking emotional experiences in patients (1959, p. 318).

When the empathizer both comprehends and accepts his own anxieties, he does not fear the contagion of the client's emotional states. He permits himself to experience more widely and more deeply what the client has experienced. He can reach beyond professional routine and reveal his own personality in a more human way to his client. Such an attitude enhances the possibility of therapeutic success. The client can recognize the reliability of the professional's understanding through his own empathies with him and is reassured by the recognition that anxious feelings threatening to him do not demoralize the professional. The client has the satisfaction of knowing that some-one else is capable of appreciating his experiences. He grows in the therapeutic meeting because he identifies with the inter-viewer who is able to accept him, even though he has experienced himself as inadequate and unacceptable.

The good therapist does not cultivate a state of anxiety within himself because of any masochistic needs. He responds to the feelings of the client, allowing them to set the course of his own feelings. He does not attempt to follow the client in his own turbulent course merely in the hope that he and the client will find the solution to mutual problems. While the participation is reciprocal, the psychological needs are not mutual by any means. The world which these two people share is the client's not the professional's world. The interview situation is therefore different from the climate of groups studied by Fritz Redl where an immediate contagion of feeling takes place because of a com-mon need (1957, p. 99). There is no such predetermined readi-ness to respond to a common stimulus in effective empathic relationships. The professional's needs are adequately met so that he is not primed unconsciously to look to his client for leadership or for sympathy. He is suggestible only because he is relaxed, open, and concerned. He is motivated only by his professional responsibilities and, as we shall note, by his genuine concern and care for the client.

A final word needs to be added about the depth and integrity of the empathizer's self-knowledge. The good counselor or therapist knows himself with exceptional penetration. He enjoys self-esteem, appreciating his strengths but also accepting his weaknesses as part of himself. There is no finality about his self-knowledge. He continues to grow in his empathies with himself. Each therapeutic experience probably deepens this self-awareness. The advantage of such inner sensitivity is that it permits him to draw freely on a wider repertory of impulses and responses. He does not shut out the stimuli emanating from his client because they threaten to open up unsolved problems of his own. He has learned to listen to himself without excessive fear and therefore is capable of listening to signals from the client that may be anxiety provoking. The novelist James Baldwin with simple directness pointed to a human reality which we take to be critical for effective empathy: "The questions which one asks oneself begin, at last, to illuminate the world, and become one's key to the experience of others. One can only face in others what one can face in oneself. On this confrontation depends the measure of our wisdom and compassion" (1961, pp. xiii-xiv).

The Swiss psychiatrist, Alphonse Maeder made a similar observation regarding the physician who can "take his patient only as far as he himself has gone" (1953, p. 187). The effective empathizer goes far in his self-scrutiny; he learns to trust himself to the outer limits of his own emotional capacities. What keeps him from stopping prematurely in empathizing are his courage and his self-esteem.

Eros and Objectivity

In this section we shall discuss the role of the practitioner's positive feelings for his client, the quality of such feeling, and the issue of involvement and positive countertransference.

We begin with the assumption that the interviewer requires some form of *energy* for his empathic activity. This is necessary whether he uses empathy primarily for understanding or for establishing a supportive relationship as well. In the humanities, in art, literature, and the theater there is more agreement than in psychology and the social sciences regarding the urgency of such personal feelings in empathy.

The empathizer requires an intense, personal motivation to comprehend the feelings of another person in depth. He must first of all be able to resist the temptation of other interests and problems which make calls upon his attention. In order to clear the channels of his imagination, he must be able to give up or at least suspend other projects which already absorb his energies. It is not easy to set aside other interests in which he is already involved. Another reason why empathic activity makes unusual emotional demands is that the practitioner must often overcome a certain inertia he may feel when trying to comprehend some feelings which often appear to be irrational and confusing. It is easier to empathize with individuals who experience physical suffering. The therapist's eyes can immediately take in the signs of their discomfort so that some kind of involvement is almost immediate as soon as the visual stimulus is received. Psychological difficulties, in addition to being obscure and shadowy, are contagious. If the client experiences anxiety, he may convey a vague restlessness and puzzling agitation which invade the therapist's emotional being. Something unknown and nameless presents itself, and the therapist must be able to overcome the initial tendency to withdraw and reject what may be distasteful if not actually anxiety provoking to him as a human being.

Energy is needed also for the therapist's imagination to begin to deal with evanescent and unseen experiences. What Gregory Zilboorg once wrote about the involvement necessary for understanding historical figures is appropriate to the interviewer as well:

one must mobilize, not anesthetize, one's feelings, revitalize all strivings, even weaknesses and passions; otherwise it will be totally impossible to put one's self in the place of Alexander the Great or Jesse James or Cromwell or Julius Caesar or the humblest slave of ancient Rome (1941, p. 18).

The past comes alive for the historian who can release such emotional powers within himself. The client in the interview becomes more real and more fully present to the counselor or therapist in the same way. Under the influence of stronger feelings, the empathizer will appreciate more keenly the experiences of the client. The "heat" generated by such personal or subjective investment must always be subject to control and must frequently be alternated with the coolness of distance and detachment; the energy must be available, subject to control but intense enough to move the empathizer into the position of the other person and stir his imagination into creative activity. The empathizer must be motivated to associate to the intangible and the mysterious. He needs energy to persevere when he must work without instruments and complete objective evidence and to draw on his own emotions, never being fully in command of them nor completely defended against the discomfort they might evoke. He has the support of his clinical knowledge and his experience with other clients, but each new client in some ways is a fresh challenge and he must begin to empathize *de novo* in every case. Even after the initial trial identification, he must again and again rely on his own fund of energy for additional acts of empathy and for moving in and out of his identifications.

According to Theodor Reik, the therapist has a ready store of energy for empathic penetration of others because each act of empathy reflects the basic desire of the ego to understand itself. The energy is automatically available because the ego has a built-in instinct to seek to comprehend itself (1949, p. 422). Reik's theory can be understood in the light of our earlier discussion on primordial empathy. The therapist's desire to understand himself carries over into a desire to understand others because he is fundamentally related to others and any increase in understanding of his fellows gratifies his need for self-understanding. It is likely that something more than this basic drive for self-understanding is required for the task of the professional empathizer. To persevere through long years of difficult experience in comprehending the egos of others, requires a care for others which will continually energize him.

Even scientific curiosity, powerful as it is, cannot supply the quality and consistency of emotional drive that the good empathizer needs. He requires the propelling force of a need to take in the experience of others and a *controlled passionate concern* for their growth and self-realization. The desire to understand himself and objects in his environment must be supplemented by an active involvement and a readiness to share. The sociologist Charles Cooley has provided us with a most pertinent psychological explanation of the nature of this energy:

To go out into the life of other people takes energy, as everyone may see in his own experience; and since energy is limited and requires some special stimulus to evoke it, sympathy becomes active only when our imaginations are reaching after something we admire or love, or in some way feel the need to understand and to make our own (1922, p. 155).

However, Cooley adds an important qualification. The good empathizer requires not only energy but energy of a kind that flows from an active concern. Such a positive attitude is a necessary condition for the initial act of empathy; it is a common experience to find that subsequent identifications with a client generate an even stronger attachment.

Something more must be said about our affection or "love" for the client. If this were no more than a gambit in therapy, representing a conscious and superficial attempt to achieve a proper therapeutic relationship, less energy would be required. If the empathizer merely simulates an attitude, he involves less of himself. He would likely not communicate with the other person in any depth and would evoke shallow feelings in his client, because depth of feeling in one tends to correspond with the depth of feeling in the other. In the case of the effective empathizer, identifications are vital and energetic, reflecting as they do a genuine investment of feeling in his client. He is fully *present* to his client because he is propelled out of his professional detachment and his private inertia by a love for his client that is real, though controlled.

The effective empathizer accomplishes most when he experiences care for his client and responds with some degree of the intensity and involvement he might feel for a member of his own family or for a personal friend. No doubt he can go far in psychological understanding, stimulated as he might be by a sense of professional responsibility and by his strong scientific curiosity. But deeper communication calls for genuine investment of personal feelings in his client. Martin Buber commented that the doctor can do "repair work" without the form of empathy he calls "inclusion," but to "regenerate an atrophied personal core, the healer must take the role of an active partner" (1958b, p. 133).

Even negative or hostile feelings are capable of energizing the empathizer. They connect him with his client and yield empathic awareness of qualities and realities that otherwise might have been missed. Hostility in the therapist does not establish a supportive relationship nor does it by any means make possible a balanced and complete identification with the client; but it is often capable of probing areas closed to the neutral observer. Hostility is helpful in appreciating the vulnerabilities and resentments of the client. The therapist may succeed in detecting his client's hostilities through an empathic identification made possible by his own negative and destructive feelings. He may have a talent for uncovering pathology. His own weaknesses and conflicts make him notice what other observers might overlook. He recognizes and identifies in others some problems of his own. It is not likely that he is conscious of the reasons for such keenness in diagnosis. The data that he uncovers is useful if it corresponds to realities in the client and is not just a matter of the interviewer's neurotic projection.

Positive feelings play an important role in diagnosis or research as well as in the actual work of counseling or therapy. The therapist who is propelled by positive feelings toward himself and toward others is more likely to be sensitive to the potential strengths and assets of his client. This does not mean that he refuses to recognize the morbidity of his client. He is simply more open to the possibilities of growth. He does not find what he projects. He penetrates to an actual inner core of health. Like the sensitive friend in the hasidic parable translated by Martin Buber, the good therapist knows both the faults and the needs of the other because of his love:

[The Rabbi] sat among peasants in a village inn and listened to their conversation. Then he heard how one asked the other, "Do you love me, then?" And the latter answered, "Now, of course, I love you very much." But the first regarded him sadly and reproached him for such words: "How can you say you love me, Do you know, then, my faults?" And then the other fell silent, and silent they sat facing each other, for there was nothing more to say. He who truly loves knows from the depths of his identity with the other, from the root ground of the other's being he knows where his friend is wanting. This alone is love (1958a, pp. 248-249).

We are so strongly influenced by the psychoanalytic discoveries about the distortions of love—positive countertransference in the language of that specialty—that we find it difficult even to imagine what realistic positive interest might be in the therapist-client relationship. Popular terms like interest, care, concern, attachment, mutuality, friendship, or loving-kindness suggest themselves. Certainly it is not a brooding, enveloping sentimentalism, nor a moralistic, do-gooder orientation, and certainly not a feeble and impractical humanitarianism. It is not a diffuse affection nor a clamorous concern.

The sensitive practitioner enters into a live and spontaneous relationship which is marked by recognition of the client's worth, by responsiveness to his problems, and by faith in his potentialities. His positive feeling must grow out of his increasing knowledge of the client, for if it were not based on personal knowledge, it would not be love for the specific person. The most gifted therapist is likely to experience more positive feelings with some clients than with others, but he is capable of entering into sensitive relationships with a larger variety of individuals than can the less richly endowed empathizer. His imagination embraces more of the depth and range of the other's experience and his participation in the feelings of others is more active. He has an almost inexhaustible patience with his clients, and the steady confidence he has in them is communicated to them and generates self-confidence. The therapist reaches this depth of participation, writes Edith Weigert, "only if he gives up the illusion of artificial neutrality and becomes fully aware of his emotional reactions" (1961, p. 192). Izette de Forest, an American interpreter of the ideas of Sandor Ferenczi, maintains that empathy depends on the wish to be of loving service and a readiness to be lovingly touched by the sufferings of others. "One can gain *insight* into another's problems and one can be intuitive without this extension of loving care but one does not experience empathy without it" (1960).

Mrs. de Forest also speaks of the movement from empathic examination to "the final give and take with the patient, as a person of equal emotional vigor" (1954, p. 123). We must now ask whether the loving attitude of the practitioner is reciprocated by the client. To some extent high empathy depends on mutuality, and in good therapeutic relationships the client develops positive feelings for the interviewer that are not entirely a matter of transference. The client often regains his capacity for love as a result of investing positive feelings in his therapist, but he is not likely to have the personal knowledge of his therapist that would lead realistically to the intimate and loving relationships he has with lifelong friends or family. It is only natural that the client reveal more of himself and that the interviewer alternate between empathic involvement and professional detachment. The professional is under no obligation to match the self-revelations of his client with his own. Were he to do this and burden the client with his problems, he would do harm to the client, to say nothing of abusing a professional relationship. The love of the counselor or therapist for the client is analogous to the love of the parent for the child—it is protective and solicitous, although the relationship is not that of equals and the child has or should have few if any responsibilities for the parent. The therapist invests love and patient care in his client but does not expect emotional gratification in return. Try as he may to make the therapeutic interview human and sensitive, he recognizes that the client is in a dependent position and that he cannot, even if he were to try, reciprocate the care of the professional. Carrying the family analogy further, the therapist can be seen as a father to several children, tempering his care for one with his responsibilities for others, and working toward the ultimate goal of helping each child achieve independence and become capable of being a parent himself. Martin Buber has used the analogy of the master-pupil relationship in discussing the limits of mutuality in therapy. The teacher lovingly includes the experience of his pupil in his own, but it is essential that the pupil, in turn, not experience the same complete "inclusion" (or empathy in our term) with the teacher.

the specific "healing" relation would come to an end the moment the patient thought of, and succeeded in, practising "inclusion" and experiencing the event from the doctor's pole as well. Healing, like educating, is only possible to the one who lives over against the other, and yet is detached (1958b, p. 133).

The good therapist is therefore one who participates most actively and lovingly in a relationship yet finds it possible to reconcile such loving identification with a minimum of the professional status he must retain. A certain amount of one-sidedness is inescapable because the meeting with the client which has to rise to the level of friendship must still be subject to the limits of an agreement, professionally arranged, in which one party seeks help from another who is qualified to give it.

The kind of love or positive feeling discussed here calls for lively interaction between the practitioner and the client. It is spontaneous, human, and personal. As such it is not the same phenomenon psychoanalysts describe as "positive countertransference." Edith Weigert—herself a psychoanalyst—has suggested that the therapist's emotional attitude can be more than a transference reaction. It can amount to an active sympathy which also differs from passive empathy: ". . . it is a part of this value-enhancing love, capable of envisioning the personality of the patient in his potential wholeness, even though this wholeness may at present be only adumbrated, obscured by a preponderance of destructive processes from which he seeks liberation" (1961, p. 192). The good empathizer is able to relate to the specific client whom he faces as a real and unique individual and the involvement he feels is far from a projection of feelings carried over from his own childhood or from his own familial relationships. It is not a regressive movement back to identifications out of the therapist's past, echoes of which are reactivated by contact with the client. Obviously some elements of the professional's biography will enter in and influence his attitudes to the client. But such positive feelings as he may have for the client grow out of his current interaction with him and represent part of a human meeting or encounter. They are realistic, here-and-now responses to specific clients and to actual qualities in those clients.

The positive feelings for the client which we suggest are characteristic of the good counselor or therapist may include the positive countertransference which the psychoanalysts sometimes acknowledge as being useful in therapy. The therapist may be reminded of a figure in his childhood or in current personal relationships outside of therapy and carry over into his therapeutic attitude some of the affection and personal involvement he actually experiences vis-à-vis another person. It is true that the client may often benefit from such a warm attitude on the part of the therapist, even though that attitude does not reflect the actual personal engagement of the therapist with him as a specific individual. But not all positive feeling on the part of the interviewer vis-à-vis his client is transference. He is also capable of relating to his client as a fellow human being. Even though the situation in which he meets his client calls for professional controls, it is still a meeting or a social encounter and there is room for realistic feeling that does not merely reflect the shadows of the therapist's past identifications. In the model of the counselor or therapist that we are presenting, the relationship of therapist and client is a human relationship, the engagement between them is social, and "real love" for the client is often critical for healing. We need have no uneasiness about using such a common and human term as "love" if we are not inflexibly and unreasonably committed, as are some psychiatrists, to a rigorous and classic model of a scientific laboratory in which an object is tested and manipulated by an expert who by definition must be dispassionate and by personal preference chooses to be impersonal.

The professional does not simulate an affection for the client, if he happens not to experience it before and during his empathic relationship. The pretense of a friendship, apart from being unethical, often backfires because the client can discover his therapist's actual feelings. On the other hand, when the therapist's friendship is real, the client will sooner or later appreciate its genuineness and will identify with it to his advantage.

Because the next chapter deals with the hazards and failures in empathy, we mention only briefly some of the risks, particularly the dangers of involvement and love, to which the good therapist is alert. His awareness of such hazards does not paralyze him, and his distinctive skill consists in walking a narrow line between proper and improper use of positive feelings. He knows, for example, that positive feelings for the client may interfere with making objective diagnoses. There is the possibility that he may reject certain evidence or impressions that would yield a diagnosis of acute mental illness because the thought of such a disability in a person close to him would be painful. He is protected against such distortions or blind spots because he has already gained considerable self-knowledge and constantly re-examines his own reactions, checking them by objective and realistic standards. (It goes without saying that therapists with negative feelings toward clients, either conscious or unconscious, are capable of overlooking strengths and of overemphasizing or misinterpreting the evidence for pathology.) He knows too that his benevolent concern for the patient may interfere with the progress of therapy. He may try too hard because of his involvement, pushing the patient too quickly, and stressing too much certain signs of recovery. This "therapeutic furor," as Freud called it, is not inevitable when the therapist is actively involved. It may in fact represent a lack of genuine love for the patient and reflect, instead, the therapist's need to prove his virtuosity as a healer. The experienced and qualified therapist who uses empathy is equipped with checks and balances which guard him against such errors in practice. If his concern for his patient is genuine, he does nothing that would bring his client harm.

The skillful counselor or therapist recognizes also that expressions of his concern for the patient and indications of his intentions to support him in some degree are capable of frightening some who cannot tolerate the show of affection. What positive feelings he has for the client, he controls objectively and communicates at those times and to those degrees that are appropriate to the emotional state of his client. Such caution and reserve are not as essential with individuals who have the ego strength which the more disturbed person lacks. But even in more spontaneous relationships with individuals who are capable of more give-and-take, the therapist is careful to observe the effects of his positive feelings. He is able to recognize that certain steps which the client takes reflect more of a desire to please the therapist than an objectively valid step forward to increased health and independence. He is alert to the possibility that the client will improve through what the psychoanalysts call a "transference cure" or a "flight into health."

Here again, it is the therapist's real concern for the welfare of his client that protects him from being deluded by superficial progress. His respect for his client is too great to allow him to misread the signs of health or ill-health. At times he may even increase the anxiety level of his client because he recognizes that the expression of his positive involvement may mislead the client into thinking that someone else will solve his problems for him. It is not a case of the therapist granting or withholding measured dosages of affection for the client. The relationship cannot be so easily manipulated. What is characteristic of the good counselor or therapist is his ability *to involve himself actively without losing sight of objective danger signals.*

VI

MISSING THE MARK

THE EFFECTIVE empathizer succeeds in getting an inside appreciation of his client. He also helps his clients to change. He tends to have repeated experiences of attaining similarity to his clients. He participates quite fully in their worlds. At the same time he shows himself to be adept in balancing his participation with his detachment, walking a narrow ridge between excessive empathy and myopic objectivity. There are times when his empathies are less reliable and less profound, but, generally speaking, he is competent in the use of his subjective processes.

In turning our attention to the practitioner who misses the mark, we must note that he does not commit gross errors in empathizing. We should not equate him with the layman whose mistakes in empathy often indicate neurotic trends. His errors and blind spots are far less obvious. What he misses in his communication with clients as a group or what he fails to apprehend in his relationship with a particular client is a subtle shading of feeling, a nuance of emotion, a finer quality of relationship. He misses making contact in the fullest possible human way. He may face his client, but he cannot be said to *be* there fully.

Even though his failures in empathy are far from gross when contrasted with his clients' failures in communication, they are serious in their consequences. Often the success of therapy depends on the rare moments of direct and empathic communication. When such moments do not emerge in the relationship, the communication is not completed. The client does not feel that he is understood; the therapist himself recognizes that much as he is familiar with the client and his inner world, the core of the client has escaped him and he is left baffled in his attempts to understand and to help. What distinguishes therapeutic from ordinary communication is the degree of penetration into inner and extremely private meanings. It is the establishment of an openness of relationship. When the practitioner fails, he has not participated intimately enough in the emotions of his client. On the other hand, the participation may have been so engrossing and so irreversible that the practitioner overidentifies with the client and disqualifies himself for the disinterested analysis that is necessary.

Although models are helpful in ordering our thinking, they tend to overstate the case. We must therefore take care in counterposing to the model of the effective empathizer, a type or a series of types whom we would label as deficient, inadequate, inconsistent, or excessive empathizers. Each of these terms points up some failing in empathy and helps account for reasons why practitioners would miss the mark. We hesitate to set up a model of empathic failure: even the effective empathizer has moments of less than complete empathy, while the therapist with less than spectacular success with the general run of his patients occasionally finds it possible to achieve a high degree of empathy with a particular patient or in a particular interlude in a relationship that is otherwise unproductive. So many variables bear on the success or failure of empathic union between two individuals that it is next to impossible to generalize, to identify a given practitioner as being a consistently versatile and effective empathizer, or to identify another as being consistently deficient in empathic powers. Much depends on the *matching* of the particular client and the particular counselor or therapist. Nathan Ackerman reminds us that "some pairs click instantly and others fail regardless of long effort" (1958, p. 267). Even with this caution in mind, it seems reasonable to conclude that some therapists fail more frequently than others. Given the same random selection of clients or patients, they have fewer experiences of empathic pairing.

Even though we do not intend to present a unitary model of the professional who misses the mark in empathy, we shall use certain labels to identify the empathizers who fail and to dramatize the degree and the direction of their failure. Social psychologists who make empirical studies of empathy by interviewing and testing cross-sections of laymen supply us with several helpful terms. They use such terms as these to classify subjects who scored low on empathy tests: projectors, self-derogators, authoritarians, ethnocentrics, fundamentalists, or hyper-conformists. While we lack evidence of the scores that therapists might make on such empathy tests, we would conclude that their deviation from the norm would be far less significant. Nevertheless, they do experience empathic failures which, though subtle, are quite real and definitely subversive in their therapeutic work. When they do experience such failures it is likely that in some degree they partake of the same qualities which account for the grosser errors in empathy scored by the low empathizers. Counselors and therapists tend to project, to derogate clients because of their own self-derogation, to gloss over individual differences because of their own tendencies to conform, and to miss taking the role of the other because of their needs to dominate. The same mechanisms are at work; it is a question only of degree.

To these categories of the social psychologist, we might add the following which describe the blind spots of the professional:

"the marginal empathizer"	penetrates only to a part of the client's experience. Is selectively inattentive.
"the evangelical or apostolic empathizer"	aggressively therapeutic. So concerned with changing the client he fails to empathize with the client as he is.
"the hysteric empathizer"	overidentifies in a symbiotic way.

"the compulsive empathizer"   identifies with one ego state of
                               the client but cannot easily shift
                               his identifications.

"the rationalistic empathizer" underidentifies. Cannot abandon
                               his professional role or permit
                               himself to regress.

Most errors in empathizing are determined by personal
anxieties of the individual therapist. He over- or underidentifies
because of his own needs, conflicts or problems. This is the individual equation on which we shall comment later in the chapter.
Even though empathy itself is basically a psychological process,
there are situational and structural forces which tend to shape its
course. Some of the errors of the practitioner of empathy derive
from cultural and professional blind spots. Even the most empathically sensitive therapist must still deal with the limitations of
being bound to a particular culture and of being indoctrinated
in the conventions of a particular status or profession. However,
the greater his empathic powers the less likely he is to become
vulnerable to such prejudices of his profession and the less apt
he is to become rigidly attached to these conventions and
precedents. The more secure he is as an individual, the less will be
his need to use his professional status as a defense against the
challenge or the contagion of his client's problems. Allowing
even for individual variations in the response to situational and
cultural roadblocks to empathy, we must still recognize that the
temperament and training of the individual are not the only
variables in successful empathy. There are built-in hazards and
situational complexities which must be identified and dealt with
by the therapist even should he have the native empathic powers
of Shakespeare or the penetration of Freud. The more modestly
endowed practitioner can greatly expand his empathic range by
becoming more alert to professional and cultural blinders.

Decline in Native Empathic Power

The professional empathizer has first of all the situational
limitation of being an adult in whom some decline in empathic

powers seems inevitable. Such a loss is not critical for the average person who becomes a conventional member of society and communicates efficiently enough for his purposes. The therapist, who requires a high degree of sensitivity because of the depth of the communication he needs to establish with his client, is handicapped by any decline in his capacity for new imagery and for spontaneous experience.

While some natural decline is irreversible, it is important for the therapist to be aware of the fact that his empathic powers quite normally are diminished by the force of convention. He may become vulnerable to stereotypes and to an erosion of spontaneity and depth of feeling. The researches of Ernest G. Schachtel into the imagery of the adult and variations in perception and sensation have indicated how pervasive are the differences in sensation between the adult and the child. It is not that the adult becomes the victim of certain conventions and habitually relies on stereotypes. He actually loses some of the earlier intensity of his memory, so that it has an "incapacity to reproduce anything that resembles a really rich, full rounded, and live experience" (1949, p. 11). Schachtel goes far in reminding us of the empathy variable between the adult and the child. "The adult is usually not capable of experiencing what the child experiences; more often than not he is not even capable of imagining what the child experiences" (1949, p. 11).

Schachtel's explanation of this constriction of empathic powers helps us to appreciate blind spots in the empathy of the professional. The child is more fully open to his environment and has less need to control and to manipulate. He is eager for experience and is not coerced by inner needs and by convention to select and to discriminate among the people and the objects with which he will identify. He is playful and experimental. The adult, on the other hand, focuses on specific and conscious goals, and practices selective inattention to qualities in objects for which he has no immediate use. He has only the tunnel vision which he requires for navigating the route which is already determined.

For the practitioner even to recognize that his powers of empathy have been narrowed in the process of education and maturation is some gain. More important than the healthy skepticism that would lead him to check his impressions is the courage he might have to keep something of the child alive in him. He requires an appreciation of the playfulness and non-direction of the child's fantasy. This is more than becoming tolerant of a moment of regression, indulged in almost guiltily. It is part of the self-respect of the therapist which calls, when necessary, for the fullest disregard of convention and for a willingness to approach another person as innocent as possible of any desire to coerce him. Only the child enters the kingdom of heaven and who knows but that only the therapist with child-like empathies can open the door on the troubled lives of his clients.

The Wall of Anxiety

There are personal factors too which tend to make the therapist miss the mark in empathy. His fears, his unmet needs, and his own unsolved personal problems have the effect of raising a wall of anxiety which separates him from his client.

The range of the therapist's empathy is subtly restricted because, like the layman, he tends to project, to over- and under-identify. His insecurity, his excessive rigidity or excessive plasticity of ego boundaries, and his own narcissism invade and distort the empathic relationship. Since the therapist is often not consicous of his anxiety, he has no awareness of his own interference with the process of communication.

Even with the best of intentions, we often miss the mark in empathy because our anxieties shorten and narrow the range of our feelings. We remain fragmentary or marginal empathizers. We miss sharing the rhythms of the other person's life; the spectrum of our colors does not quite match his. We do not make the full connection and the gap between us still remains, even though it has been considerably narrowed. When this happens, the client is likely to suspect that his therapist does not really participate in his world. He recognizes that he and his therapist cannot belong to the same community or appreciate common meanings and common emotions. The rebuff to the client appears slight, but its consequences are serious enough to impede the progress of therapy.

One reason for underempathizing is the temptation to detach

oneself too soon from empathic involvement. We recognize some parallels and vaguely apprehend some quality of the experience of the other and then proceed, quite without the necessary supporting evidence, to make inferences regarding the whole personality. It is a case of premature disengagement and a withdrawal of emotional energies before the meeting has actually taken place. We presume too quickly that we have overcome our strangeness and that we have understood the other person from within. We delude ourselves into thinking that we have temporarily coalesced in empathic union, but the walls still remain and important areas in the life of the other person are still unexplored. Frieda Fromm-Reichmann provided an example of a therapist who presumed that he and his patient were already friends and was soon brought up sharply by the schizophrenic patient who provided him with the ruthless and unsparing feedback that other patients are too inhibited to express.

An inexperienced psychotherapist suggested to a schizophrenic patient that he and the patient were friends. "Oh, no," the patient replied emphatically, "we are not; we hardly know each other and, besides, you want me to change; so how can you say that you are a friend of the person I am *now*" (1959, p. 154).

The empathizer who wants to become the friend of his client too often takes for granted a genuine identification that has yet to be established.

For the client the consequences of the therapist's anxiety are serious. In the first place, he finds that his therapist is either excessively cold or excessively sympathetic. Instead of meeting a genuine helper who is able to concentrate on his needs, he finds that his chosen guide is really not free to help. Second, he comes to realize that his therapist is incapable of knowing him objectively. He experiences a sense of defeat and frustration. The professional whom he originally endowed with the objectivity and authority of science proves to be a vulnerable individual, so ordinary and so fallible that trust in him and respect for his powers dissolve into a residue of bitterness. If it should happen that his therapist is unduly anxious, the client is also likely to experience an exacerbation of his anxiety.

Few therapists are immune to the threat of their own private anxieties and conflicts. Few are likely to be so secure in their profession and so fulfilled in their personal lives as to possess empathic powers that are consistently reliable and always profound and thorough. Much is made in psychoanalytic circles of the value of the training analysis of the therapist, but even such rigorous self-scrutiny and such persistent uncovering of blind spots cannot be counted on to insulate the therapist against the intrusion of personal anxieties in empathic relationships.

Freud himself suggested in his later years that insight into oneself called for constant vigilance and recommended that the analyst expose himself to reanalysis perhaps once every five years. He did not feel that the psychoanalyst enjoys a built-in guarantee of objectivity; the wear and tear of human relationships take their toll and even therapists with the most exacting professional training can lapse from their own standards: "It looks as if a number of analysts learn to make use of defensive mechanisms which enable them to evade the conclusions and requirements of analysis themselves, probably by applying them to others" (Freud, 1959b, p. 353). Others in the counseling and therapeutic professions with less training in introspection and with less supervision are at least as susceptible to errors in empathy. No interviewer, any more than any genuine artist, can neglect self-discipline and scrutiny, because the human material of his own personality is always subject to the play of forces within as well as to the influence of a constantly changing environment.

It is the anxiety of the individual professional, so often disguised and unrecognized, which makes him prone to err. It is the force which makes him project his prejudices and unmet needs on to his client, that makes him try to save his client when in fact he is intent primarily on saving himself. It is the power which pulls him back from intimacy with his client for fear that something will endanger him. He fears being possessed by the demons who already dominate his patient and who are poised within him too and ready to seize power. He would like to keep the sparks of the client's anxiety from reaching him and kindling his own anxieties into flame.

Anxiety disrupts his relationship with his client much in the same way that it disrupts the interaction of mother and child. In the words of Ernest Schachtel,

The mother can be turned fully toward the infant only if she has an attitude of tender care. Anxiety and tension disrupt such an attitude; dislike is the opposite of it. This kind of "emotional absence" of a person is familiar to our adult experience, just as we can be aware of the suppressed hostility of another person (1959, p. 51).

The client empathizes with the hostility of the therapist. Viewed from the standpoint of the therapist, it means that he is shut off from the experience of his client. He is emotionally absent himself and soon his client will take his leave as well, recognizing that he has been rebuffed. The conversation may continue but it is polite talk between strangers and no more. It is important to recognize that anxiety may move the empathizer in opposite directions—toward an excess or toward a deficiency in intimacy. In either case he becomes a stranger to his client and empathy goes wide of the mark.

The ever present problem in empathy is the danger of projecting oneself into the world of another and then neglecting to respect the integrity and separateness of the other. Where the effective empathizer merges with his client and then detaches himself for the purpose of objective evaluation, the more anxious empathizer is so preoccupied with himself and with his own needs that he fails to recognize that differences still remain between him and his client, no matter how intense the feelings of similarity or identification. He is in danger of substituting himself for his client and of erasing the actual boundary that exists between them. Erich Fromm has described a narcissistic orientation in which the individual "experiences as real only that which exists within oneself, while phenomena in the outside world have no reality in themselves" (1956, p. 118). This is a failure in reality-testing and derives from the anxiety of the individual who enjoys no self of his own that is independent of others. Narcissistic projection cuts off the vision of the therapist. He can see only himself, his values, and his needs when in fact he should be apprehending and evaluating the world which belongs to the client. We are indebted to John Cohen for this appropriate quotation from Plutarch's Life of Alexander:

King Darius had offered Alexander ten thousand talents and certain territories as ransom for prisoners of war. Parmenio, the friend of Alexander, advised his master thus: "If I were Alexander, I would accept this offer," to which Alexander replied, "So would I if I were Parmenio" (1958, p. 135).

Parmenio, who was incapable of empathizing with Alexander, had only imposed his needs and received the appropriate rebuff for his lack of objectivity. Counselors and therapists who on occasion must give advice, are susceptible to the same kind of distortion.

The anxiety-ridden projector moves into the world of his client because he sees himself in everything. It is anxiety, too, which impels some individuals to gratify their own needs by vicariously living the lives of others. This is the other face of the same coin. If one has unmet needs for affection or has no adequate self of his own, he is capable of abusing his relationship with others. Empathy may be a means of achieving personal satisfaction; the client exists in such a situation for the pleasure of the professional. There is a hidden desire to enjoy the client, a predisposition to benefit from the experiences of others which are different and perhaps more exciting than one's own. The psychiatrist who hears a patient discuss a happy courtship, wrote Frieda Fromm-Reichmann, may project because of his own unmet needs:

The psychiatrist, having in mind the lack of glamour in his own life, may use the patient's account as one might use fiction or screen romance, as a starting point for fantasies of his own, projecting himself into the role of the patient or of the patient's partner instead of concentrating exclusively upon listening to the patient in his own right (1959, p. 66).

Such self-indulgence diverts attention from the client. The therapist is likely to misinterpret the meaning of the experience he has empathized. The boundaries of private need and professional responsibility get mixed and the patient is cheated of the insights he had a right to expect from his therapist. Even though the professional empathizer is trained to avoid overidentifying, he is not always above such vicarious pleasures. The more adequate his own family life and the more vigilant his own sense of professional ethics, the less frequent and the less impulsive will be such moments of self-indulgent fantasy. He is subject to over-identification with his client when he is not firmly established in his own values. He is, in fact, exploiting his patient (Weigert, 1961, p. 194).

The more secure the practitioner, the less he has to fear his client. The more rooted in an identity of his own, the less he will be tempted to project himself into the client's experiences as an envious imitator. The private world of the empathizer must have a dignity of its own, offering personal gratifications and status gratifications. If he must use the therapeutic situation to make up for the poverty of his private life, he will be taking from rather than giving to his client. Both personal ethic and professional discipline should keep him from making self-indulgent identifications.

Authoritarianism

One of the more serious hazards in the professional practice of empathy is the authoritarianism which is almost endemic to some degree. The therapist enjoys a superior position because he is the resource whom the patient consults and because it is his experience and reputation that invites the client to invest feelings of dependence in him. The emergency is something vital in the life of the client, a unique and rare experience, while for the therapist it is a matter of clinical concern. He is the expert in crises, the veteran whom it is difficult to surprise, the specialist in emotional problems who is familiar with revelations of misery and twists of fate. It is to be expected that he will not be overwhelmed by each new client and that he will preserve his equanimity when he deals with the problems of others. What so often happens is that the very expertness and authority he enjoys as a specialist and which he requires if he is to maintain himself in the stresses of his work become capable, in time, of impairing his empathy with those who are less expert and less adequate than he.

He must be a humble man to resist the temptations of a position with so much built-in authority. The more he becomes identified with his profession and the more he views himself as

the representative of a *trained elite,* the less likely he may be to
see his client as someone who is similar to him. His primary
loyalty and his deepest identification are with his own group of
fellow professionals. He has the least social distance with his
colleagues and the greatest with his clients. For this reason he
cannot, with even the best of intentions, fully overcome the
hazards of his membership in his own peer and status group. He
is inhibited from full participation or full meeting with his client.
The group he forms with his client is often deficient in the
cohesive power which we associate with empathically related
group members. He may try to make a trial identification, but
this can become no more than a gesture if he becomes too attached to his professional chair. The recently trained therapist
who is yet to feel secure in his professional identity is less apt to
be handicapped by the authoritarianism revealed by the therapist
who is an old hand in dealing with people and who becomes wise
in his own eyes when he quotes successful cases from memory.

Authoritarianism in the professional is actually little different
from the fundamentalism of the layman who scores low on empathy tests. It is rooted in the same tendency to hold rigidly to
stereotypes and to defend conventional ways of thinking and of
feeling. Lacking empirical evidence, we cannot say how prone
therapists are to this kind of professionalism. It is sufficient to
identify it as a hazard. The authoritarian demands deference
from others and is blind to his own deficiencies. Anxiety alone
cannot account for this behavior. He may suffer from unrecognized fatigue, from a relaxation of his own self-scrutiny, from a
dulling of his own sensitivities wrought by time and routine.
Clients are so much alike that he overlooks small differences.
Precedent rather than experiment becomes the guide and a mis-
placed self-confidence causes the therapist to miss the mark. What
is individual and therefore decisive for understanding is over-
looked.

Trigant Burrow recorded a personal experience which made
him sharply aware of certain built-in hazards in the therapist's
position. Something happened in the course of a therapeutic hour
which dramatized for him the therapist's vulnerability to the
attitude of the authoritarian. One of his patients had questioned
his sincerity. He requested Dr. Burrow to change positions with

him. He would take the chair of the therapist and the doctor would take the reverse position of being the patient. It was unprofessional and unorthodox, but Dr. Burrow acceded to his patient's request. Soon after yielding his own chair to the patient, Dr. Burrow gained new and painful insight into the professionalism and authoritarianism which had crept into his own therapeutic attitudes. He now recognized in himself certain tendencies toward self-vindication. *His awareness came into being only after he had changed places.* "The analysis henceforth consisted in the reciprocal effort of each of us to recognize within himself his attitude of authoritarianism and autocracy towards the other" (1927, p. xvii).

Dr. Burrow had practiced motoric or kinaesthetic empathy. But the therapist should be able to project himself imaginatively into the role of his patient and such vicarious experience should have the effect of greatly extending his self-awareness. It should help to control his incipient authoritarianism. He would be less susceptible to feelings of superiority, complacency, and dogmatism if he could step into the shoes of his client.

Empathic identification often makes possible a degree of self-adjustment. The act itself is therapeutic for the therapist. But if the therapist is solidly set in his role of authoritarian and feels himself already fortified by his superior knowledge and experience, he is likely to miss the gain in his own growth which role-taking potentially provides. Therapists often do not know how rigid they have become. They are too strongly committed to their self-images as professionals and experienced craftsmen. In such cases they lose sight of the fundamental similarity they actually have with their clients. They cannot cultivate the advantages for therapy of such similarity. They cannot extend it by imaginative reconstruction. Ultimately, they miss the mark in empathy because the particular flavor and meaning of their clients' experiences elude them.

Excessive Emphasis on Technique: The Professional Cult

One source of difficulty in empathizing effectively is the practitioner's tendency to identify himself with the fixed routines

and traditions of his profession. He feels less of a need to experiment or to involve himself as a person. Empathy calls for
flexibility and the willingness to enter into new, unprotected,
and unexplored areas. Each new client has some unique quality
which calls for a personal and unprecedented appreciation. The
therapist errs if he relies on standardized techniques or uses only
the diagnostic categories which his predecessors and colleagues
have defined for him. He must venture alone, personally and
privately, into the inner experience of another person. Even when
he has become familiar with this individual, he cannot apply a
label or a classification and feel complacent about his understanding. No other empathic relationship can be like the present
one. What gains the therapist may make in the direction of
understanding a particular individual cannot always be communicated to his colleagues. Under such circumstances he is
almost compelled, as it were, to go his own way as he establishes
the uniquely personal identification with his client. Even then
he will succeed only incompletely and can never confidently
assert that he has fully comprehended his patient. He tries to
share as fully as he can what is never completely shareable, intending to participate in that feeling which William James said
"each one of us has of the pinch of his individual destiny as he
privately feels it rolling out on fortune's wheel" (1902, p. 489).

It is not uncommon for therapists to resist the claim that
empathy is so personal and so individualistic. There is a tendency
to assert that empathic skills reflect disciplined training and can
be mastered as a matter of professional technique. What is more
important than the creative act of the individual therapist is the
application of established practices of the profession.

To be effective, the empathizer must be an individualist. He
cannot rely on his membership in the team to see him through;
his task calls for a solo flight. In his study of the professions, the
sociologist Everett C. Hughes observed that "it is as if competence became an attribute of the profession as a whole, rather
than of individuals as such" (1958, p. 141). The good therapist
would avoid such professionalism and would never cease cultivating his own powers and respecting his own spontaneity.

Some therapists admit that some of their most empathic experiences took place when they were relatively new to their profession. They were impressionable; their interests were fresh and their responses not stereotyped. Many therapists succeed in retaining the spontaneity of their formative years and add to their native abilities the insights of professional experience and continued personal growth. They achieve the vision of the poet whom Elizabeth Barrett Browning described:

> The poet has the child's sight in his breast
> And sees all *new*. What oftenest he has
> viewed
> He views with the first glory.
> *(The Poet*, 1850).

What is critical for the empathic growth of the therapist is whether he takes pride in his position in a guild or has a "dynamic image of himself as continually evolving and growing" (Ruesch and Bateson, 1951, p. 256).

The more entrenched in his profession he is, the more the therapist relies on established techniques which maintain the gulf between the specialist and the layman, between the expert and the amateur, and between the subject and the object. The person of the therapist becomes so absorbed in the professional skills that relationships become depersonalized. Often the gestures of empathic communication are made, but the reality and the freshness of the meeting are lost and in their place an almost inevitable artificiality intrudes. It is not correct to state that this professionalism is unavoidable. When and if it is found, it reflects a lack of vigilance on the part of the therapist; he loses part of his own humanity and slips into the habits of the bureaucrat for whom routine is comfortable and apparently efficient. When the professional reaches the point when he must simulate a personal interest in the client and when his identification with the client lacks spontaneity, the relationship stays fixed on one level and deeper empathy is out of the question. According to Whitaker and Malone, "Patients can always see beneath the therapist's technical skill, and if this is artificial, it becomes another barrier placed between the patient and the person of the therapist" (1953, p. 195).

Genuine empathy is impeded in any relationship when one of the partners holds on too tightly to his role of technician. This is true of the teacher who sticks too closely to formal methodology, of the parent who tries to rear his children by the book, or the poet who adheres too rigidly to the forms of a particular school and cannot communicate to his reader and establish the two-way passage of shared meanings and experiences. Often the therapist who consciously thinks of himself as unhampered by convention and free of authoritarianism is still cramped by a therapeutic manner or style which he has absorbed unconsciously from his teachers or from the particular psychological school of thought with which he has identified himself. He becomes orthodox in his practice, simply repeating the techniques he has learned. Even if he is a psychoanalyst with long years of self-study behind him, he is not immune from the dangers of routinization. He may continue to have a strong identification with the techniques of his instructors. In his own relationships with patients he is capable of overlooking the individuality of his patient, to say nothing of denying the stirrings of his own responses. The patient is reduced to a *case* to be treated by the "method."

There can really be no standard method in empathic relationships any more than we can speak of a method that can be routinely and universally applied in the creative processes of the artist or the writer. A personal engagement is necessary and while training can enhance the effectiveness of the artist as well as of the interviewer, there can in the last analysis be no substitute for the *élan* of the individual personality. Every profession has its necessary guidelines and its body of lore transmitted from one generation to another. But the apprentice must break with the master and find his own way.

The empathizer must cultivate his own individuality because failing this, he will become no more than a replica of other therapists and will be less able to enter into the empathic relationships necessary for helping his own clients. Empathy is a creative process; each client is a special case and in treating each individuality in a creative way, the therapist cannot have recourse to second-hand insights. He may receive emotional support from his colleagues and, if he is still in training, he may benefit from supervision, but in meeting the patient he enters alone. Like the creative artist, he must have the personal experience of coalescing with his subject. No one can do it for him. Formulas or techniques applied routinely are capable of stifling his own growth and of smothering the spark of genuine rapport with his client.

Some of Freud's disciples espouse a standardized technique or a stylized therapeutic attitude that may well be more orthodox than the methods of their master, who once described himself as not being a "Freudian." Whether or not the present model of the psychoanalytically oriented therapist corresponds to the actual example of Freud or whether the so-called nondirective therapists are faithful to the style and approach of Carl R. Rogers, the tendency is for therapists to take models for themselves and to adopt what they believe to be the style of the authority with whom they identify. Whatever the image may be in terms of a particular teacher of psychotherapy or a particular viewpoint in psychological theory, they assimilate themselves to it. Often they replicate it slavishly and unimaginatively. Frequently, they have less success than their masters, for in lacking the originality, they cannot adapt as flexibly and creatively. The counselor who espouses "Rogerianism" often caricatures his teacher and has little insight into the way he may be distorting Rogers' principles.

An essential point in our discussion is that the counselor or therapist finds nothing wrong in choosing a model for himself. Whether he adheres to the model accurately or whether he identifies only with a caricature of his model is not as important here as the fact that he does make a choice concerning the image of the therapist he intends to emulate. It is a human and personal act on his part, based on his recognition that the values and the style of a master are somehow essential to his own development as a practitioner. He gains an identity through this association.

Toward his clients, however, he may take a different position. Here he often tries to depersonalize the relationship. He effaces himself and discourages the client from identifying with him. He hesitates to allow a teacher-pupil relationship to develop between his client and himself and tries to maintain a position of official neutrality. Often he wishes to be not a person but a symbol to his client, not a fellow human being with whom his client might identify but a remote specialist, anonymous and detached. Therapists with such an orientation miss the opportunity of putting to therapeutic use what after all are certain given conditions of any human relationship. Whether the professional acknowledges it or not, his own personality enters into the situation.

No matter how they may duck the issue of the goals of therapy, their own ideas of heroism, their own views of what is weakness, will affect whom they accept or seek out as patients, what they say to them, and *the tacit models they themselves are for their patients* (Riesman, 1954, p. 386. Italics ours).

The personality of the therapist becomes a force in therapy because the patient identifies with him and often takes him as a model just as he, more consciously and more directly perhaps, once identified with his own teacher in counseling or psychotherapy. He may have welcomed suggestion and guidance in his own apprenticeship to his master, but he disowns the use of suggestion in therapy. Yet he cannot escape the human condition nor disentangle himself from his social encounter with the client. Much as he would like therapy to represent a kind of scientific procedure in which the personality of the particular therapist is incidental rather than significant, he cannot do this. Therapists are often unrealistic when they hesitate to involve themselves empathically because of a fear that they will cease to be scientifically neutral and that they may impose their personal values upon the client.

Their loyalty to a certain model of the scientist often blinds them to the simple fact that they are not only researchers but also change-agents. They cannot erase themselves as individuals because their values are unconcealable and the client soon recognizes them. They cannot help communicating their values. Therapeutic relationships are didactic because two human beings meet and interact. The contents of those meetings cannot be sterilized completely of personal color, feeling-tone, and value preferences.

Since feelings are bound to be communicated when two people meet, the practitioner would do well to set aside what inhibitions he may have about active empathy. Instead of ex-

pending his energies in disguising his actual identity, he might
develop his empathic powers, open himself more widely and
deeply to the contagion of the feelings of others, and develop
some skill in controlling rather than denying or totally inhibiting
his personal responses. Failing to open himself more fully, he is
likely to stereotype his responses and miss the mark in therapy.

Empathy with the Person in the Situation

There has been a growing emphasis on cultural factors in
counseling and psychotherapy. To be effective in empathizing,
it is obviously necessary to avoid the stereotypes of one's own
culture or social class, to appreciate divergent values, and to be
alert to the symbols and words which are peculiar to different
life-styles.

But it is not to the variety of situations and contexts that
we now turn our attention. We are concerned here with the
connection between the feeling and the situation. Therapists must
not only appreciate the individual in his context but also understand that feelings themselves are specific and concrete reactions
to situations and to objects and figures in those situations.

We are prone to see the energies and ego states of the individual as almost tangible entities which form part of an intact
structure we call the individual. There is a tendency to focus
attention on the "personality structure" of the individual, to
consider it almost like an archaeological site having different
layers and compartments. The individual is an object in a sealed
vacuum, a unit complete unto itself; feelings are radiations or
emanations of some core energy within. We habitually break the
connection which the individual has with his environment, with
his situation, and with the objects and persons with whom he
interacts.

Effective empathy requires that we move into the situation of
the client. This is something different from identifying with a
feeling in itself. We tend to deal with a category called feeling
and to identify with an abstraction we inherited. We may engage
in free association to certain words as if performing a semantic

drill. We may attain more precise knowledge of words but the actual emotions of the client do not come into the ken of our experience. As we observed in Chapter I, reason deals with abstractions while emotion is a charge of energy which cannot exist apart from the subject and the object. While the emotion belongs to the individual who experiences it and is registered within him, it is actually a kind of magnetic field in which both the individual and the object or situation are included. To empathize fully, the therapist must enter this larger field. He becomes involved with more than a specific individual or with an ego state within that individual. To use Kurt Lewin's terms, he enters the life-space of that individual. To be more exact, he occupies one of a series of life-spaces in a given moment of genuine empathy. The personal equation always consists of *person* plus *situation*.

The professional may take the role of his client at a specific moment when the latter interacts with his employer or when he takes the role of patriarchal authority in countering the demand of a defiant adolescent. The number of roles is extensive, and for effective empathy the therapist would have to have the facility of projecting himself into the specific role enactments or performances of the client. Viewed from this more sociological perspective, therapy itself can be seen as a technique of role clarification. The client learns more of his role expectations and explores the meaning of his situation with a therapist who has effectively empathized with him in the specific situation. The social psychologist speaking of a plurality of selves or the existentialist speaking of the "landscape" of the individual are concerned with the same phenomenon. It is a contextual approach to behavior which views emotions as connections between the individual and specific objects. Instead of empathizing with the "instincts" or "libidinal energies" of a discrete and identifiable object, the therapist enters a field of forces and merges with the total environment of his client.

Effective empathy, therefore, calls for moving into the situation of the client rather than attempting to simulate within oneself one or more of what is presumed are the intrapsychic states or zones of feeling. You do not simply listen to the pulse of feeling with an empathic stethoscope, moving the instrument from one spot to another to pick up the range and intensity of the heart beat. You are not even conscious of the rhythm of feeling as something in itself, because as a participant you are lost in the situation itself. You become an active agent in your imaginative role-play. You experience a situation, participate in a drama, and respond to live cues. The effective empathizer does not try to recapture a "feeling" as if it were an object located within the body of the client. As he feels himself into his client, he, like the client, becomes *connected* with the people and objects in the client's experience. The situation need not be current. It can be an almost forgotten experience of childhood which the client recalls. The few cues given the empathizer make it possible for him to move back in time and to occupy imaginatively the space in which this experience originally transpired. It is also possible for the therapist to accompany the client in his projections into the future and also to experience the situations—still imaginary—which have both meaning and emotional charge for the client. Feelings are inseparable from situations and from interpersonal relationships. There are as many shades of feeling as there are varieties of experienced situations. The practitioner who operates with a checklist of conventional "feelings" will never get into the individual he wishes to understand.

The following definition of "feeling" is phenomenological. It coincides with the sociological emphasis on role and situation and helps us appreciate the task of the empathizer: "Feeling is a mode of replying to a situation and transforming it as a projected new world. There are as many feelings as there are situations, and the situation is created by the mode in which I have accepted it, i.e., by my chosen projection" (Buytendijk, 1950, p. 130). The empathizer who is concerned with simulating a general or even a specific feeling is likely to miss the quality of his client's inner world unless he moves into the specific situation which the client charges with feeling and which he invests with a special significance.

The empathizer is not concerned merely with feelings labeled "sibling rivalry," "loneliness," "fear of authority," or "ambivalence." He enters into a specific situation and imaginatively places himself in the moment, in time and space when his client responded spontaneously to an event and an object. He emphasizes with the *person in the situation* and with the meanings, values, and feelings spontaneously projected in that specific context.

Stereotypes of Normality as Obstacles to Empathy

The counselor or therapist underempathizes when he yields to the frames of reference which become part of official psychological tradition. We refer to prevailing notions of psychological "normality." The modern psychologist is likely to associate himself with a *Weltanschauung* which emphasizes rationality, objectivity, and extreme deliberateness. Even if he is disposed to allow for the play of emotions in human affairs, he takes his place with the intellectual and the historian rather than with the man who decides and acts, with the participant-observer rather than with the doer. He makes tentativeness almost a virtue in itself instead of a check on the more important values of choosing and acting. Even if the therapist disowns any conscious intentions of imposing these preferences, he is likely to offer such a model of personality to his client. It is the rationalistic model which is esteemed in many professional groups. It may, however, not correspond to the needs and capacities of the individual client. So great is the prestige of the psychologist and so persuasive is the authority of "psychological science," that clients become infused with these values. They become homogenized. They gain a certain freedom, but at the same time they are prevented from developing their own powers and following their own values. Patients who have had psychoanalytic therapy sometimes give evidence of having joined a cult. As Philip Rieff wrote, "In the emergent democracy of the sick, everyone can to some extent play doctor to others, and none is allowed the temerity to claim that he can definitively cure or be cured. The hospital is succeeding the church and the parliament as the archetypal institution of Western culture" (1959, p. 355). With their former therapists and with other patients they form a "community of the saved" for whom introspection and continuous self-analysis become articles of faith. Life yields to a state of self-contemplation. Passion and spontaneity are discouraged and personal equilibrium becomes the highest value. The disciplines and exercises of the therapeutic situation become elevated to the status of a way of life.

What the therapist takes to be a self-evident value may not be relevant for a particular client. The more the therapist conforms to conventions of psychological thought the more likely he is to miss the mark in genuine empathy. Contemporary therapists who often designate themselves as followers of Freud seem far less individualistic than their model. Freud was person-centered to an exceptional degree. Although he conformed to many of the tastes and values of his day in his personal life, in his relationship with his patients he appears to have demonstrated a rare respect for the needs of the individual. He did not encourage a psychological community of patients and ex-patients who would find a common identity in their adherence to the same values. He opposed therapy by indoctrination. He believed first that it would simply not work and second that it was not appropriate for the scientific therapist to assume such a responsibility. He felt unqualified to be a seer and saw himself only as a liberator of the creative energies of the individual. He observed that others were stopping short of this individualistic ideal—the pastoral therapists drew their clients into religious communities while the Adlerian school recommended membership in the socialist fellowship. While these judgments may not be completely fair, they reflect Freud's fierce loyalty to the integrity of the individual. Contemporary therapists might well remind themselves of Freud's assertion that therapy should consist of "enriching the patient from his own internal resources" (1959a, p. 256).

Shall we say that values are completely relativistic and that the internal resources of one person are entirely different in kind from those of another? Such a view would make human values entirely anarchistic and would rule out the existence of common human needs. If we take an empathic view we acknowledge universal standards. The error we commonly make is to impose a certain version of these values and subtly but persuasively discourage the exercise of initiative and spontaneity by the individual. The therapist often ends by evoking a new kind of conformity. Freud's trenchant criticism of this trend is classic:

> Our object will not be to rub off all the corners of the human character so as to produce "normality" according to schedule, nor yet to demand that the person who has been "thoroughly analyzed" shall never again feel the stirrings of passion in himself or become involved in any internal conflict (1959b, p. 354).

The "evangelical empathizer" is confident that his values and his conceptions of what is normal are valid for himself and for all of his clients. He is more attached to his categories than to his clients; each convert he makes will vindicate his judgment and will eventually proselytize on behalf of the master's teachings. The therapist expects his own status to be enhanced if he gains more disciples. In the end he displays increasingly less respect for the integrity of the individual. He may continue to invoke psychological science as a support, but he has in fact ceased to be scientific because he no longer questions his own assumptions. He has invested too much of himself in his categories and has too little energy left to pay attention to the individual, to his temperament, to his needs, and to his capacities for distinctive and original thinking.

The empathic therapist would have less need to make disciples or establish a church. He would have the more mature gratification of helping another person grow. He would be the catalyst for the unfolding of a personality. Such a role would give him some narcissistic pleasure at no cost to the patient. More significantly, he would have the sense of fulfillment enjoyed by the parent who knows that his child has grown to self-reliant and independent adulthood. Therapists like parents must learn to "let go" and to give up the ambition to surround themselves with facsimiles of themselves.

Preoccupation with social conventions and private preferences blocks empathy in two ways: It interferes with objective research and it undercuts genuine understanding. The ineffectual empathizer is not open to the new and the unknown because he sees only further examples of the principles or category he already knows. He cannot liberate the client because he does not care enough for the client as a person with rights of his own.

VII

EMPATHY AND ETHICS

OUR PRESENTATION of empathy hinges on the principle that we comprehend those whom we resemble. We already share a basic similarity with our fellow man. In the moment of empathy our sense of similarity or identity is made more intense and more vivid. We participate in the experience of our fellow man to the fullest possible degree. We descend from the Eiffel tower of the observer. We surrender the aseptic and sharp detachment of the scientist, breaking with his ethic which has traditionally insisted on a suspension of personal interest and emotional involvement. It is true that we alternate between merger and detachment, moving in and out, as it were, of our engagement with the other person, but it cannot be denied that our empathic activity reduces the distance between ourselves and our subjects.

Even at those moments when we disengage ourselves and try to get the perspective of psychic distance in order to evaluate the client, we do not become so dissimilar or so unrelated that we think of the client as a thing and not a person. We are men who try to understand and to help others who are made of the same stuff and spirit as we. We can never escape this simple reality.

Because empathy calls for greater use of subjective processes, it requires more ethical controls than other more consistently objective methods of research, communication, and therapy. Who will check on the imaginative activity of the therapist? His empathy with his client is not subject to the usual standards of objective measurement. How completely has he avoided projecting his own values or substituting his own experiences for the experiences of the client with whom he identifies? The non-verbal, inner experience of the therapist, like that of the client, is not entirely shareable and therefore is not available for checking or for comparison. The experiments of the empathizer cannot be repeated step by step by outsiders. Errors and distortions cannot therefore be checked as easily as in the physical sciences, in mathematics, or logic. Since he is himself part of the prescription [the term is Michael Balint's], his own person being a pharmacological agent, the therapist must have unusual purity of motive. There is no intermediary between his client and himself, no machine whose reading is open to anyone who would examine it, no chemical compound whose combination of ingredients can be objectively analyzed. He applies no formulas which have been validated.

Since the empathizer participates in the experience of another person by allowing the flame of his conscious self to burn low, he becomes vulnerable to the excesses and distortions of feeling at the same time that he becomes capable of understanding more vividly and immediately because of his emotional involvement. If his respect for himself and for his client is not securely anchored he will drift from one identity to another. How is it possible to become so deeply involved and yet hold on to one's own identity? How can one invest both conscious and unconscious mental activity and yet be sure of an ultimate and complete control of one's attitudes and feelings, once this deep investment has been made? These questions are difficult, but answers can be found when the empathizer is himself a person of integrity who is willing and able to take a risk for the sake of helping another person.

The discomforts of involvement are so great that we can appreciate why many counselors and therapists hesitate to engage in anything more than perfunctory or superficial empathy. They use better judgment than those who recklessly involve themselves in relationships that can be destructive as well as uncomfortable.

Freud recommended "emotional coldness" as the most suitable therapeutic attitude and urged that therapists take the surgeon as their model of disinterested concentration. One basis for this recommendation was his conviction that such an attitude was best for the patient. But another reason, at least as important and perhaps more so, was his persistent concern with the human weaknesses of the therapist. "Our control of ourselves," he wrote, "is not so complete that we may not suddenly one day go further than we had intended" (1958, p. 164).

The patient or the client can be seen as the lamb exciting the wolf to attack. The reverse is possible too; the therapist who would be gentle and loving can be devoured by the rapacious, instinct-ridden patient. Erotic involvement is seen as an ever present danger. The patient is always a potential temptation to the therapist, a sexual object capable of throwing him off his chosen course. The patient may also be an object of sympathy or pity who can reduce the therapist to a helpless participant, defenseless against a flood of fellow feeling. With therapists so susceptible and with clients so irresistibly seductive and provocative, there could be no alternative but an armed neutrality. In this view, the therapist is a perfectionistic moralist. He will place himself beyond temptation and above the shadow of suspicion.

Freud's caution conveys ethical and philosophic implications we must question. Those who restrain and inhibit spontaneous empathy because they doubt their own powers of self-control must consider whether or not they are really facing the need of the patient. The therapist's concern about doing harm to the patient is always legitimate. But the therapist has to face the ethical question also. Does he elect to take a position of emotional coldness because it is safer? Is his decision dictated by

the actual requirements of the treatment situation? The therapist
has to scrutinize himself and determine as honestly as he can how
far he may be rationalizing an anxiety about getting close to
people.

The concern about loss of self-control and fears of investing
emotion raise another issue. It concerns the philosophy of man
or the nature of human nature.

There is a recurrent theme in some psychoanalytic sources
which suggests that human relationships are exploitative and
predatory to a far greater degree than those uninitiated into the
mysteries of the unconscious can possibly realize. One man requires another for his gratification. One's fellow is not so much a
fellow creature, a member of the same group with whom one
has a natural affinity, but an object which is available for the
purposes of tension-release and exploitation. Fellow feeling or
love is suspect, since we can never be sure that benevolence and
care are anything more than disguises of lust or self-interest.
Since love is likely to be a reaction formation against a more
primary emotion of aggression, therapists who invest positive
feeling in their relationships could conceivably be sadists in dis-
guise. Pursuing this theme to the ultimate, it could be said that
the therapist is motivated only by a desire to defend himself
against destructive impulses when and if he extends love to his
client. Were he perfectly honest and completely scrupulous, he
would, in the name of morality and truth, refrain from offering
love which cannot be sincere. There is some allowance for the
power of Eros in the world, but this theme emphasizes the
predominance of aggressive and hostile instincts.

Objective evidence supporting a particular conception of
human nature is hard to find. Our theories of human nature are
themselves often projections of our interpersonal attitudes. Even
theories offered in the name of science reflect *a priori* values;
their ethical level is by no means higher than the level of theories
of man which derive from poetry, theology, or metaphysics.
Certain positivistic and mechanistic theories of human nature may
likely falsify and distort because quite irrationally and unjustifi-
ably, they do not allow for nonmaterial and spiritual dimensions
in human nature.

A different orientation concerning man and society suggests a different ethic. Being human means more than being a physico-chemical unit. To be a man means to be a fellow man. The human personality becomes *human* through its association with others. Man fulfills himself in human relationships. He has instincts for affiliation as well as for destruction. His need for affective communication with others is at least as primary as the impulse to devour and destroy. In the light of this view of man, another ethic is appropriate in defining the grounds of the therapeutic relationship.

The hostile and exploitative impulses are not so explosive or irreversible as we imagined and not every human relationship is so loaded with temptation. Both the therapist and the client are capable of defining roles; the therapist is fully capable of maintaining ethical limits if the patient is still deficient in this ability. The intimacy and fellow feeling that develop in empathic relationships neither endanger the therapist's security nor violate his ethic. It is possible for one individual to be identified with another and be concerned for his welfare without thought of private gain. Disinterest in terms of personal pleasure is compatible with emotional involvement in the world of the other person.

It is true that the therapist may derive a certain private or narcissistic gratification out of his efforts on behalf of his client, but even this element of self-interest does not invalidate the objective and ethically proper concern he has for that client.

Even if we are to say that objective love is not possible and that fundamentally every act of care for another person is only care for the self we project into others, we are still capable of giving acceptance that is significant to that other person. If all love is self-love, it could be said that humanity is really one, that empathy reflects the primordial unity in which all were originally part, and that our similarity is really based on actual identity. Even the biblical ethic concerning loving one's neighbor as much as one loves himself supports this theme. One interpretation even holds that we love our neighbor *because* he is like us! Baeck has given a somewhat different rendition of Leviticus 19:18, usually translated "Thou shalt love thy neighbor as thyself." The exact translation in his opinion would read, "Thou shalt love thy other; *he is as thou*" (1950, p. 20. Italics ours). Metaphysically the basis of empathy is a belief in the brotherhood of man. Every individual is created in the image of God and therefore is innately similar to his fellows. This ascribed empathy is reinforced by the Divine commandment "Thou *shalt* love!" (Leviticus 19:18). The philosopher George H. Mead has observed that those who put themselves in the attitude of others for nonexploitative reasons engage in a fundamentally religious act. He has distinguished between those who empathize for the purpose of selling an unwanted object and those who concern themselves with the objective welfare of the other person:

The religious attitude, on the contrary, takes you into the immediate inner attitude of the other individual; you are identifying yourself with him in so far as you are assisting him, helping him, saving his soul, aiding him in this world or the world to come—your attitude is that of salvation of the individual (1934, pp. 296-297).

A built-in similarity or biological empathy between one person and another provides the ethical basis for empathy in therapeutic relationships. The therapist who actively identifies with his client does more than heighten and intensify what is a basic affinity in one human being for another. The therapist is actually not so different from his patient, no matter how troubled or unfulfilled that patient may be. He has the same endowment, the same impulses, and has shared many of the same human experiences. He should be able to regard his client as a fellow creature, a friend, an individual similar to himself in whose welfare he is involved humanly as well as professionally.

What, then, motivates the therapist? It is his own humanity and the sense of mutuality he feels natively and instinctively for a friend. It is this self-less concern which is mixed with but not spoiled by a personal desire to be professionally competent. The therapist does not have to arm himself against an inevitable temptation to victimize the client or protect himself against the contamination of his client's anxieties. The tabu on tenderness, which is not uncommon among therapists, derives from the fear that the show of feeling is weakness. The proper state of man, of the therapist as well as of the patient, is a stoic, independent, self-reliant isolate. A man must be well defended at all costs.

An alternative view, perhaps equally difficult to support on empirical grounds, holds that one man is part of another and that acceptance and mutuality are more normative for man than are detachment and indifference. The nonempathic therapist takes a basically human meeting and dehumanizes it. In the empathic relationship, however, both therapist and patient learn how to be true to themselves. When they meet, the integrity of their relationship is all the greater if they are fully present to each other. The therapist, who is the more active empathic partner in the dialogue, finds that his involvement elicits feelings of altruism for his client. He finds also that his conscience is sharpened by empathy. After taking the role of his client, he has a stronger appreciation of the ethical and psychological truth that he is his brother's keeper. His client is a client only for a moment but a fellow human or a brother always; their common humanity makes it so.

At the core of empathy is ethical concern for the sacredness of the individual. The client stands as a unique and idiosyncratic universe, related to others in so many respects yet qualitatively different in other respects. The therapist respects the integrity of each client. He avoids violating the right of the individual to develop his own nature. The ethics of empathy are therefore abused when the brainwasher or thought-reformer empathizes with his prisoner. He pretends to give the victim a new sense of liberation, but the goal of his invasion of the victim's privacy is the annihilation of individuality in favor of brutish conformity to the state.

The ethics of empathy are violated also when the empathizer aims only to adjust the individual to social patterns or to ideologies and attitudes. Such empathic activity alienates the individual from his own freedom and from the essence of his own personality. Genuine empathy is far more individualistic. The therapist enables the client to discover new dimensions in himself, but he does not insinuate personal and conventional values with the ethical claim that these are objective or normal.

The therapist requires ethical standards of his own which

derive from the integrity of his own self-knowledge and self-acceptance. As he experiences himself honestly and openly as far as it is possible for him to do so, he will be able to experience the world of his client more profoundly and more confidently. He continuously examines his own personality so that this empathic instrument is not agitated by anxiety or blunted by routine. He is required to cultivate his own individuality because only as a person can he be most valuable to his fellow man. He must be capable of attuning himself to rhythms of feeling and nuances of meaning in the experience of others. For this he requires the capacity for spontaneous response, for fresh and child-like sensitivity and wonderment. The more he is alive as a person, the more open he is as a friend, the more courageous he is as a therapist—the greater will be his gift of empathy to his client.

The counselor or therapist who is capable of offering empathic understanding offers a human service that is increasingly rare in human relations. An experience of genuine and objective empathy is uncommon because our society grows more bureaucratic, less respectful of the dignity of the individual and less tolerant of private freedom and spontaneity. In some cases even the advantages of empathy are used by the practitioner to violate the basic rights of the individual. Agents of institutions and political powers misuse the insights gained from empathic interviews. They aim to enforce conformity and are as ready to use empathy as any other technique in order to manipulate the individual. Such practitioners have surrendered their own integrity.

A police detective may empathize with an accused criminal in order to get inside information. But his use of empathy could be justified. He protects society and may save the accused himself from self-destructive acts. In cases of brainwashing, however, empathy is used in sadistic and predatory ways. By putting himself in the position of the political prisoner, the agent of the state discovers human vulnerabilities. He manipulates and entraps his victim. He may even make a show of respect for his prisoner, identify with him, and simulate a concern for his welfare. But he remains an antagonist and he finally violates the personality of his fellow man. His use of empathy repels us, but we know now how effective it can be in securing information and changing attitudes when ordinary persuasion or actual physical intimidation have failed. Experts in motivation research have been ingenious enough to apply empathy to uncover the suppressed needs of potential consumers and gain insight into their wishes and conflicts. Such insight can then be sold at a profit to would-be vendors of merchandise. Even though such researchers do far less violence to human dignity than do the brainwashers and could conceivably be said to play a necessary role in the economy, they are not motivated by an objective concern for individuals. They have no professional restraints or moral commitments keeping them from exploiting empathic techniques.

The scientist who uses empathy to extend the frontiers of scientific knowledge uses empathy more ethically. This is equally true of those counselors and therapists who do more than work at a trade. When he establishes an empathic relationship with a client, the therapist indicates that for him the client is a person and not an object. He identifies with a fellow human being. He meets with an individual who is unique by nature and by experience. The client is not interchangeable with another person and has a right to be accepted for what he is and for what he may choose to become. The fact that the therapist is willing to enter into an empathic relationship with a patient for many months and often for years is in itself an act of nonconformity. We are accustomed to making men subordinate to institutions and to grinding down the margins of individuality. That so many individuals require the services of empathic counselors may be a symptom of the sickness of an increasingly alienated society. The demonstration of unqualified respect for individuals by the counselor or therapist is a symbolic protest against the values of a mass society.

The therapist *qua* therapist cannot solve the problem of an alienated society. He is not qualified to prescribe the changes in the social structure that are necessary in order to remove the causes of alienation. He cannot even prescribe a way of life for the individuals who come to him for psychological assistance. The empathic relationship he establishes with the client must by its very nature be provisional and limited. The client ultimately takes leave of his therapist and finds his place in an impersonal society where he lives on his own resources. The contribution that the counselor or therapist makes is to give his client an experience of empathy and acceptance. Such genuine empathy helps the client realize more of his own freedom. It helps him mobilize his energies to cope more adequately with what ultimately are common human problems in a mass society where men tend to be estranged from each other and estranged from themselves (C. Wright Mills).

We close this survey of empathy, its origins and nature, its uses and misuses, with this quotation from the late Rabbi Leo Baeck. His words account for the origin of empathy and point up the challenge for those who would use it in helping relationships.

To be a man means to be a fellow man. I am to make the man beside me my fellow man by my will and my deed. By my choice and my duty I must make a reality in life what is already reality through God. . . . The other man is my fellow because God made him such, and yet my deed is to make him a fellow man to me! That which is becomes a commandment (1948, p. 195).

REFERENCES

Ackerman, Nathan W. 1958. *The Psychodynamics of Family Life*. New York: Basic Books.

Adler, Alfred. 1927. *Understanding Human Nature*. Translated by Walter Beran Wolfe. New York: Greenberg.

Alexander, Franz. 1960. *The Western Mind in Transition*. New York: Random House.

Baeck, Leo. 1948. *The Essence of Judaism*. Translated by Irving Howe. New York: Schocken.

———. 1949. "The Interrelations of Judaism, Science, Philosophy and Ethics." Cincinnati: The Hebrew Union College-Jewish Institute of Religion.

Baldwin, James. 1961. *Nobody Knows My Name*. New York: Dial Press.

Bartlett, F. C. 1932. *Remembering*. Cambridge: Cambridge University Press.

Bates, Walter Jackson. 1956. *From Classic to Romantic*. Cambridge, Mass.: Harvard University Press.

Bergson, Henri. 1911a. *Creative Evolution.* Translated by Arthur Mitchell. New York: Henry Holt.
———. 1911b. *Laughter.* Translated by C. Brereton and F. Rothwell. New York: Macmillan.
Blitsten, Dorothy R. 1953. *The Social Theories of H. S. Sullivan.* New York: William Frederic Press.
Bowen, Catherine Drinker. 1959. *Adventures of a Biographer.* Boston: Little, Brown.
Briffault, Robert. 1921. *Psyche's Lamp.* London: George Allen & Unwin.
Buber, Martin. 1948. *Between Man and Man.* Translated by Ronald Gregor Smith. New York: Macmillan.
———. 1953. "Distance and Relation." Translated by R. G. Smith. *Psychiatry.* Vol. 16.
———. 1958a. *Hasidism and Modern Man.* Edited and translated by Maurice Friedman. New York: Horizon Press.
———. 1958b. (1923). *I and Thou.* Second Edition. Translated by Ronald Gregor Smith. New York: Charles Scribner's Sons.
Burrow, Trigant. 1927. *The Social Basis of Consciousness.* London: Kegan Paul, Trench, Trubner & Co.
Buytendijk, F. J. J. 1950. "The Phenomenological Approach to the Problem of Feelings and Emotions." In *Feelings and Emotions.* Edited by Martin L. Reymert. New York: McGraw-Hill.

Cameron, Norman. 1947. *The Psychology of Behavior Disorders.* Boston and New York: Houghton Mifflin.
Cohen, John. 1958. *Humanistic Psychology.* London: George Allen & Unwin.
Collingwood, R. G. 1958. (1938). *The Principles of Art.* New York: Oxford University Press.
Cooley, Charles Horton. 1922 (1902). *Human Nature and the Social Order.* New York: Charles Scribner's Sons.
———. 1926. "Kinds of Knowledge." *American Journal of Sociology.* Vol. 32.
Coutu, Walter. 1951. "Role-Playing vs. Role-Taking: An Appeal for Clarification." *American Sociological Review.* Vol. 16, No. 2.

Darwin, Charles. 1955 (1872). *The Expression of the Emotions in Man and Animals.* New York: Philosophical Library.
De Forest, Izette. 1954. *The Leaven of Love.* New York: Harper.
———. 1960. Letter to author dated February 26, 1960.
De Unamuno, Miguel. 1954 (1921). *The Tragic Sense of Life.* Translated by J. E. Crawford Flitch. New York: Dover.
Dewey, John. 1910. *How We Think.* Boston: D. C. Heath.
Downey, June E. 1929. *Creative Imagination.* New York: Harcourt, Brace.

Dresner, Samuel H. 1960. *The Zaddik*. New York: Abelard-Schuman.
Dymond, Rosalind F. 1948. "A Preliminary Investigation of the Relation of Insight and Empathy." *Journal of Consulting Psychology*. Vol. 12.

Erikson, Erik H. 1950. *Childhood and Society*. New York: Norton.
———. 1957. "The First Psychoanalyst." In *Freud and the 20th Century*. Edited by Benjamin Nelson. New York: Meridian Books.

Farber, Leslie. 1957. "What Is Effective in the Therapeutic Process?" *American Journal of Psychoanalysis*. Vol. 17, No. 1.
Federn, Paul. 1952. *Ego Psychology and the Psychoses*. New York: Basic Books.
Fenichel, Otto. 1945. *The Psychoanalytic Theory of Neurosis*. New York: Norton.
Ferenczi, Sandor. 1927. *Further Contributions to the Theory and Technique of Psychoanalysis*. Compiled by John Rickman. Translated by J. I. Suttie. New York: Boni and Liveright.
———. 1955. *Problems and Methods of Psycho-Analysis*. Edited by Michael Balint. New York: Basic Books.
Fliess, Robert. 1942. "The Metapsychology of the Analyst." *The Psychoanalytic Quarterly*. Vol. 11, No. 2.
Foulkes, S. H. and E. J. Anthony. 1957. *Group Psychotherapy*. Harmondsworth, Middlesex: Penguin.
Freud, Sigmund. 1933. *New Introductory Lectures on Psycho-Analysis*. Translated by W. J. S. Sprott. New York: Norton.
———. 1943. *A General Introduction to Psycho-Analysis*. Translated by Joan Riviere. New York: Garden City Publishing Co.
———. 1953 (1905). "On Psychotherapy." In *The Standard Edition*. Vol. 7. Edited by James Strachey. London: Hogarth Press.
———. 1955a (1919). "Lines of Advance in Psycho-Analytic Therapy." In *The Standard Edition*. Vol. 17. *Ibid.*
———. 1955b (1921). *Group Psychology and the Analysis of the Ego*. *The Standard Edition*. Vol. 18. *Ibid.*
———. 1955c (1923). "Psycho-Analysis." In *The Standard Edition*. Vol. 18. *Ibid.*
———. 1957a (1914). "On Narcissism: An Introduction." In *The Standard Edition*. Vol. 14. *Ibid.*
———. 1957b (1915). "The Unconscious." In *The Standard Edition*. Vol. 14. *Ibid.*
———. 1958 (1915). "Observations on Transference-Love." In *The Standard Edition*. Vol. 12. *Ibid.*
———. 1959a (1926). *The Question of Lay Analysis*. In *The Standard Edition*. Vol. 20. *Ibid.*
———. 1959b (1937). *Analysis Terminable and Interminable*. In *Col-*

lected Papers. Vol. 5. Edited by James Strachey. New York: Basic Books.

————. 1959c (1926). "Address to the Society of B'nai B'rith." In *The Standard Edition.* Vol. 20. *Ibid.*

————. 1961 (1930). *Civilization and Its Discontents.* In *The Standard Edition.* Vol. 21. *Ibid.*

Fromm, Erich. 1947. *Man for Himself.* New York: Rinehart.

————. 1950. *Psychoanalysis and Religion.* New Haven: Yale University Press.

————. 1956. *The Art of Loving.* New York: Harper.

Fromm-Reichmann, Frieda. 1950. *Principles of Intensive Psychotherapy.* Chicago: University of Chicago Press.

————. 1959. *Psychoanalysis and Psychotherapy.* Edited by Dexter M. Bullard. Chicago: University of Chicago Press.

Gottschalk, Louis. 1945 (with Clyde Kluckhohn and Robert Angel). *The Use of Personal Documents in History, Anthropology, and Sociology.* Social Science Research Bulletin, No. 53.

Hughes, Everett Cherrington. 1958. *Men and Their Work.* New York: The Free Press of Glencoe.

James, William. 1902. *The Varieties of Religious Experience.* New York: Modern Library.

Katz, Robert L. 1959. "Empathy in Modern Psychotherapy and in the Aggada." In *Hebrew Union College Annual.* Vol. 30.

Kelley, George A. 1955. *The Psychology of Personal Constructs.* New York: Norton.

Köhler, Wolfgang. 1959 (1938). *The Place of Value in a World of Facts.* New York: Meridian Books.

Lerner, Daniel. 1959. "Social Science: Whence and Whither?" In *The Human Meaning of the Social Sciences.* Edited by Daniel Lerner. New York: Meridian Books.

Levine, Maurice. 1961 (1952). "Principles of Psychiatric Treatment." In *The Impact of Freudian Psychiatry.* Edited by Franz Alexander and Helen Ross. Chicago: University of Chicago Press (Phoenix Books).

Lipps, Theodor. cf. Rader, Melvin M.

Lorenz, Konrad Z. 1961 (1952). *King Solomon's Ring.* New York: Thomas Y. Crowell (Apollo Editions).

Low, Barbara. 1935. "The Psychological Compensations of the Analyst." *International Journal of Psychoanalysis.* Vol. 16.

Lumeij, J. L. J. 1957. *The Methods of Psychology and Psychiatry.* Assen, Netherlands: Van Gorcum.

McKellar, Peter. 1957. *Imagination and Thinking*. London: Cohen and West.

Maeder, Alphonse. 1953. *Ways to Psychic Health*. Translated by Theodore Lit. New York: Charles Scribner's Sons.

Maranell, Gary M. 1959. "Role Taking: Empathy and Transparency." Unpublished doctoral thesis. Ames: State University of Iowa.

May, Rollo, Ernest Angel, and Henri F. Ellenberger (eds.). 1958. *Existence: A New Dimension in Psychiatry and Psychology*. New York: Basic Books.

Mead, George H. 1934. *Mind, Self and Society*. Edited by Charles W. Morris. Chicago: University of Chicago Press.

Menninger, Karl. 1958. *Theory of Psychoanalytic Technique*. New York: Basic Books.

Moreno, Jacob L. 1953. *Who Shall Survive?* Beacon, N. Y.: Beacon Press.

———. 1956 (1914). *Progress in Psychotherapy*. Edited by J. L. Moreno and Frieda Fromm-Reichmann. New York: Grune & Stratton.

Murphy, Gardner. 1947. *Personality*. New York: Harper.

Murphy, Lois Barclay. 1937. *Social Behavior and Child Personality*. New York: Columbia University Press.

Rader, Melvin M. 1935. *A Modern Book of Esthetics*. New York: Henry Holt.

Redfield, Robert. 1955. *The Little Community*. Chicago: University of Chicago Press.

Redl, Fritz. 1957. Quoted in *Group Processes*. Edited by Bertram Schaffner. Transactions of the Third Conference on Group Processes. Josiah Macy, Jr. Foundation.

Reik, Theodor. 1949. *Listening with the Third Ear*. New York: Farrar, Straus and Company.

Rieff, Philip. 1959. *Freud: The Mind of the Moralist*. New York: Viking Press.

Riesman, David. 1954. *Individualism Reconsidered*. New York: The Free Press of Glencoe.

Rioch, Janet MacKenzie. 1949. "The Transference Phenomenon in Psychoanalytic Therapy." In *A Study of Interpersonal Relations*. Edited by Patrick Mullahy. New York: Grove Press.

Rogers, Carl R. 1954. "Some Hypotheses Regarding the Facilitation of Personal Growth." Unpublished paper read April 22, 1954, at Oberlin College.

Rokeach, Milton. 1960. *The Open and Closed Mind*. New York: Basic Books.

Ruesch, Jurgen, and Gregory Bateson. 1951. *Communication*. New York: Norton.

Schachtel, Ernest G. 1949. "On Memory and Childhood Amnesia."
In *A Study of Interpersonal Relations*. Edited by Patrick Mullahy.
New York: Grove Press.
———. 1959. *Metamorphosis*. New York: Basic Books.
Schafer, Roy A. 1959. "Generative Empathy in the Treatment Situation." *The Psychoanalytic Quarterly*. Vol. 28.
Scheler, Max. 1954 (1913). *The Nature of Sympathy*. Translated by
Peter Heath. New Haven: Yale University Press.
Sullivan, Harry Stack. 1953. *The Interpersonal Theory of Psychiatry*.
Edited by Helen Swick Perry and Mary Ladd Gawel. New York:
Norton.
———. 1954. *The Psychiatric Interview*. New York: Norton.
Suzuki, D. T. 1960 (with Erich Fromm and Richard de Martino).
Zen Buddhism and Psychoanalysis. New York: Harper.

Tönnies, Ferdinand. 1940 (1887). *Fundamental Concepts of Sociology*. Translated by Charles P. Loomis. New York: American Book.

van Kaam, Adrian L. 1959. "The Feeling of Being Understood."
Journal of Individual Psychology. Vol. 15, No. 1.

Watson, David Lindsay. 1953. *The Study of Human Nature*. Yellow
Springs: Antioch Press.
Weber, Max. 1949. *The Methodolgy of the Social Sciences*. Translated and edited by Edward A. Shils and Henry A. Finch. New
York: The Free Press of Glencoe.
Weigert, Edith. 1961. "The Nature of Sympathy in the Art of Psychotherapy." *Psychiatry*. Vol. 24, No. 3.
West, Morris L. 1959. *The Devil's Advocate*. New York: William
Morrow.
West, Rebecca. 1928. *The Strange Necessity*. New York: Double Day
Doran.
Wheelis, Allen. 1958. *The Quest for Identity*. New York: Norton.
Whitaker, Carl A., and Thomas P. Malone. 1953. *The Roots of Psychotherapy*. New York: Blakiston.

Zilboorg, Gregory. 1941 (in collaboration with George W. Henry).
A History of Medical Psychology. New York: Norton.
Zweig, Stefan. 1962 (1932). *Mental Healers*. Translated by Eden and
Cedar Paul. New York: Frederick Ungar.

BIBLIOGRAPHY

Books

Adler, Alfred. 1956. *The Individual Psychology of Alfred Adler.*
Edited by H. L. Ansbacher and R. R. Ansbacher. New York: Basic
Books.

Alexander, Franz. 1948. *Fundamentals of Psychoanalysis.* New York:
Norton.

Allport, Gordon. 1937. *Personality.* New York: Henry Holt.

Balint, Michael. 1957. *The Doctor, His Patient, and the Illness.* New
York: International Universities Press.

Beardsley, Monroe C. 1958. *Aesthetics.* New York: Harcourt, Brace.

Burns, C. Delisle. 1923. *The Contact between Minds: A Metaphysical
Hypothesis.* London: Macmillan and Co.

Bychowski, Gustav, and Louise J. Despert. 1952. *Specialized Techniques in Psychotherapy.* New York: Basic Books.

Coutu, Walter. 1949. *Emergent Human Nature.* New York: Knopf.

Earle, William. 1955. *Objectivity*. New York: Noonday Press.

Fromm, Erich. 1955. *The Sane Society*. New York: Rinehart.
Fry, Roger. 1920. *Vision and Design*. Harmondsworth, Middlesex: Penguin.

Gill, Merton, Richard Newman, and Frederick C. Redlich. 1954. *The Initial Interview in Psychiatric Practice*. New York: International Universities Press.
Goffman, Erving. 1959. *The Presentation of Self in Everyday Life*. New York: Doubleday Anchor Books.
Groos, Karl. 1901. *The Play of Man*. Translated by Elizabeth L. Baldwin. New York: Appleton.

Kropotkin, P. 1914 (1902). *Mutual Aid*. New York: Knopf.

Langbaum, Robert. 1957. *The Poetry of Experience*. London: Chatto and Windus.
Lippitt, Ronald, Jeanne Watson, and Bruce Westley. 1958. *The Dynamics of Planned Change*. New York: Harcourt, Brace.

McGill, V. J. 1954. *Emotions and Reason*. Springfield, Ill.: Charles C Thomas.
Maucorps, P. H., and R. Bassoul. 1960. *Empathies et Connaissance d'Autrui*. Monographes Françaises de Psychologie III. Paris: Centre National de La Recherche Scientifique.
Morris, Charles. 1955. *Signs, Language, and Behavior*. New York: George Braziller.

Polanyi, Michael. 1958. *Personal Knowledge*. Chicago: University of Chicago Press.

Rogers, Carl R. 1951. *Client-Centered Therapy*. Boston: Houghton Mifflin.
Ruesch, Jurgen, and Weldon Kees. 1956. *Nonverbal Communication*. Berkeley: University of California Press.

Spencer, W. Wylie. 1930. *Our Knowledge of Other Minds*. New Haven: Yale University Press.
Stewart, David A. 1956. *Preface to Empathy*. New York: Philosophical Library.
Strauss, Anselm (ed.). 1956. *The Social Psychology of George Herbert Mead*. Chicago: University of Chicago Press (Phoenix Books).

Tauber, Edward S., and Maurice R. Green, 1959. *Prelogical Experience*. New York: Basic Books.

Van Den Berg, J. H. 1955. *The Phenomenological Approach to Psychiatry.* Springfield, Ill.: Charles C Thomas.

Vivas, Eliseo, and Murray Krieger. 1953. *The Problems of Aesthetics.* New York: Rinehart.

Wild, K. W. 1938. *Intuition.* Cambridge: Cambridge University Press.

Articles

Abel, Theodore. 1960. "The Operation Called Verstehen." In *The Structure of Scientific Thought.* Edited by Edward H. Madden. Boston: Houghton Mifflin.

Allport, Gordon W. 1954. "The Historical Background of Modern Social Psychology." In *Handbook of Social Psychology,* Vol. I. Edited by Gardner Lindzey. Cambridge, Mass.: Addison-Wesley.

Aring, Charles D. 1958. "Sympathy and Empathy." *Journal of the American Medical Association.* Vol. 167.

Blackman, Nathan, Kathleen Smith, Robert J. Brockman, and John A. Stern. 1958. "The Development of Empathy in Male Schizophrenics." *The Psychiatric Quarterly.* Vol. 32.

Bruner, Jerome S., and Renato Tagiuri. 1954. "The Perception of People." In *Handbook of Social Psychology,* Vol. II. Edited by Gardner Lindzey. Cambridge, Mass.: Addison-Wesley.

Cameron, Norman. 1951. "Perceptual Organization and Behavior Pathology." In *Perception: An Approach to Personality.* Edited by Robert W. Blake and Glenn V. Ramsey. New York: Ronald Press.

Fromm, Erich. 1957. "Man Is Not a Thing." *The Saturday Review.* March 16, 1957.

Gompertz, Kenneth. 1960. "The Relation of Empathy to Effective Communication." *Journalism Quarterly.* Vol. 37., No. 4. Bibliography of sixty-five items.

Hutchinson, Eliot Dole. 1949. "Varieties of Insight in Humans." In *A Study of Interpersonal Relations.* Edited by Patrick Mullahy. New York: Grove Press.

Ichheiser, Gustav. 1949. "Misunderstandings in Human Relations." *American Journal of Sociology.* Vol. 55, No. 2.

Klein, D. B. 1932. "Scientific Understanding in Psychology." *Psychological Review.* Vol. 39.

Kluckhohn, Clyde. 1959. "Common Humanity and Diverse Cultures."
In *The Human Meaning of the Social Sciences.* Edited by Daniel
Lerner. New York: Meridian Books.
Kohut, Heinz. 1959. "Introspection, Empathy, and Psychoanalysis."
Journal of the American Psychoanalytic Association. Vol. 7, No. 3.

Lowie, Robert H. 1960. "Empathy or Seeing from Within." In *Culture in History.* Edited by Stanley Diamond. New York: Columbia
University Press.

Maslow, Abraham H. 1948. "Cognition of the Particular and of the
Generic." *Psychological Review.* Vol. 55.
Miller, David L. 1946. "The Meaning of Explanation." *Psychological
Review.* Vol. 53.

Sarbin, Theodore, R. 1954. "Role Theory." In *Handbook of Social
Psychology,* Vol. I. Edited by Gardner Lindzey. Cambridge, Mass.:
Addison-Wesley.
Stewart, David A. 1954. "The Psychogenesis of Empathy." *The Psy-
choanalytic Review.* Vol. 41.
Stewart, David A. 1955. "Empathy, Common Ground of Ethics and
Personality Theory." *The Psychoanalytic Review.* Vol. 42.

Vidich, Arthur J. 1955. "Participant Observation and the Collection
and Interpretation of Data." *American Journal of Sociology.* Vol.
60, No. 4.

Zeleznik, Carter. 1957. "The Role of Empathy in Science: Measurement and Control." Kylos. *International Review for Social Sciences.*
Vol. 10.

INDEX